My Folks Rode the Rails

Edited by:

Vicki Schalansky
and
Traci Smith

Topeka, Kansas

Ora J. R. Bontrager
3440 N 200 E.
LaGrange Ind.
46761

A Good Book to read.

Published by Ogden Publications
1503 SW 42nd St., Topeka, Kansas 66609

For more information about
Ogden Publications titles,
or to place an order, call:
(Toll-free) 1-800-678-4883.

ISBN 0-941678-70-9
First printing April 2001
Printed and bound
in the United States of America

Photo credits:

p. vi	Chris Cruz
p. 2	Chris Cruz
p. 24	Kansas State Historical Society
p. 38	Kansas State Historical Society & Chris Cruz
p. 60	Kansas State Historical Society & Chris Cruz
p. 108	Kansas State Historical Society & Chris Cruz
p. 120	Kansas State Historical Society
p. 142	Chris Cruz
p. 154	Chris Cruz

All Aboard!

The most famous train of all
May be the Wabash Cannonball,
Or the train that carried Roosevelt
With pleated velvet walls.

Oh how I envy Bergman
Upon the Orient Express.
Can't forget the Canadian Pacific
Held down by London at his hobo best.

There is excitement to be found by ship
Out upon the open sea,
And if time is of the essence,
It's upon a plane I'll be.

But if you wish to travel in style
My friend, steel rails are calling thee,
So All Aboard! Ye adventuresome wiles,
Come ride the train with me.

– William Edwards

Dedicated to the people who established the railroad in the United States and maintained it for decades as a primary means of transportation and information.

Although it seems a lifetime ago, it hasn't been that long since trains were the country's lifeline. They provided transportation for mail, freight and people. Their arteries and spurs reached into virtually every community across the nation, and they provided employment for many people.

With the advent of the interstate highway system and air travel, the use of trains diminished and with it the romance of rail travel. Our intent in compiling the stories in this book is to preserve the memories of railroads for future generations, who won't know what life was like when railroads united the nation.

A common sentiment expressed in the letters can be found in the words of Eddie V. Bales of Mulvane, Kan.: "I worked for the Rock Island Railroad for 10 years, and I enjoyed every minute of it. I loved each and every experience there. After leaving the railroad, I went back to school and became a pharmacist. Still, I have never really gotten those steel rails out of my blood."

The lonesome wail of the train whistle and the clickety-clack of the wheels against the rails are sounds that evoke nostalgia for many Americans with steel rails in their blood. Their stories will take you into another era.

– The editors

Contents

Chapter 1
Working on the Railroad

Free train rides

I worked in the Freight Receipts Office of the Great Northern Railway in St. Paul, Minn., in the 1940s. It was a fortunate thing for me, because I got passes to ride Great Northern trains. On a trip to Glacier National Park on the Empire Builder, I saw the Rocky Mountains for the first time. I also took several weekend trips to Winnipeg, Canada. Another time, a co-worker and I went to Seattle for a week. We had to pay for our berths on the Pullman car of the Oriental Limited, otherwise the trip was free, except for food in the dining car. When we wanted to go to Chicago for a long weekend, we got half-fare passes on the Zephyr or The 400.

On the job, I operated a comptometer – a calculating machine, which is now obsolete. The amount of iron ore or coal had to be multiplied by the cost per ton to ship it.

After I married and became a stay-at-home mom, the Great Northern merged with another railroad and became the Burlington Northern Railroad. By then, my husband and I had bought a car and didn't travel by train anymore. I must say, I loved working for the railroad, and the free trips were nice bonuses. Now, 50 years later, I still think about my trips by train.

In 1999, my oldest granddaughter and I took a train ride. She had never ridden on a train before, and she thoroughly loved it. For me, riding the restored Empire Builder really brought back memories.

Lucille A. Anton
Circle Pines, Minn.

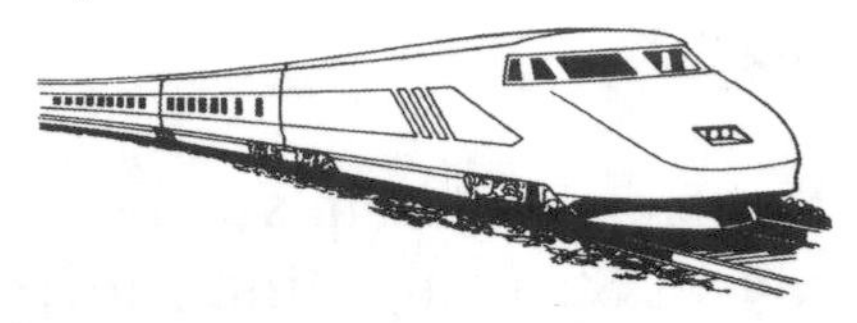

Railroad blood runs deep

My love affair with trains began when I was a young girl. We lived in Hoisington, Kan., and my dad worked for the Missouri Pacific Railroad, which ran through town for more than 40 years. The shop whistle sounded the workday for the community.

I remember how exciting it was to be lifted into the cabs of those huge locomotives, and I never missed a chance to wave to the engineers and other trainmen on the caboose. They almost always responded with a wave, and sometimes with a toot. I still wave today. I guess railroad blood really does run deep.

Since it was a railroad division point, all trains changed crews and engines in Hoisington. During the World War II years, when the troop trains stopped, word quickly spread among the teen-age girls. Troop trains were easily identified by a white flag on the front of the engine.

One of the best things about Dad working for the railroad was the pass, which allowed the family to ride free. We also had access to a foreign pass, which allowed us to ride free on any railroad. A trip to the New York World's Fair in 1940 was a freebie, and transportation to college in Emporia, Kan., never cost a dime.

I married a man who shares my love of railroads, and we have ridden from coast to coast with our two daughters. With trains few and far between, and living some distance from Amtrak, all I have now are my memories of the railroad days.

Alberta Robb
Pittsburg, Kan.

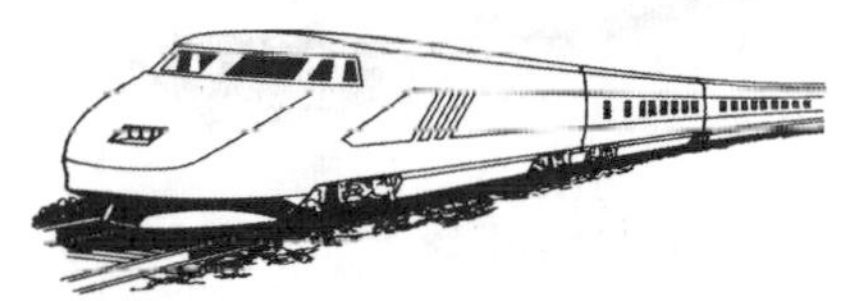

My father's secret code

My father worked for the railroad for about 45 years. Most of those years were spent as a telegrapher and office clerk doing bills of lading.

My father not only worked around trains, he loved them. Our old home movies are full of train scenes, pictures of old steam engines, views of trains moving through snowstorms or under sunny skies. If we were out for a drive in our '36 Chevy and had to wait for a train, it didn't bother my father. In fact, he had some way of sounding the Chevy's horn as a signal to the engineer that he was also involved with trains.

After my father passed away, my sisters and I gave many of his mementos to a nearby town, where the Shawmut Historical Society is located. Today, under a glass case, in an old railroad car, my father's things are displayed – a shovel once used to put coal into an engine, a railroad lantern, old bills of lading, books of railroad rules and snapshots of my father standing beside a locomotive.

If he can see all of this, he must be overjoyed. He loved the railroad!

Joan Stephen
Portville, N.Y.

Unexpected visitors

As a 12-year-old boy, my father worked for Canadian Pacific Railway. The job sent him trudging three miles from his home near Scotstown, Quebec, to the nearest siding of the railroad. There he filled switch lamps with kerosene, trimmed the wicks and made sure the signal lights were burning for the night trains.

Sometimes the temperature dropped to 35 or 40 degrees below zero, but Dad strapped on his snowshoes and made the trip every afternoon. He didn't mind putting in the time and effort needed. After all, $8 a month was a lot of money in 1907.

He did mind, however, two adult wildcats he encountered one day on his way to work. He saw them, dropped his oil can in the snow, fled home and got his father to fill in for him. Those wildcats caused my dad's employment with the railroad to end abruptly. He did not hesitate to give it up for a less scary job, that of second cook for a lumber camp.

Vi Johnson
Fullerton, Calif.

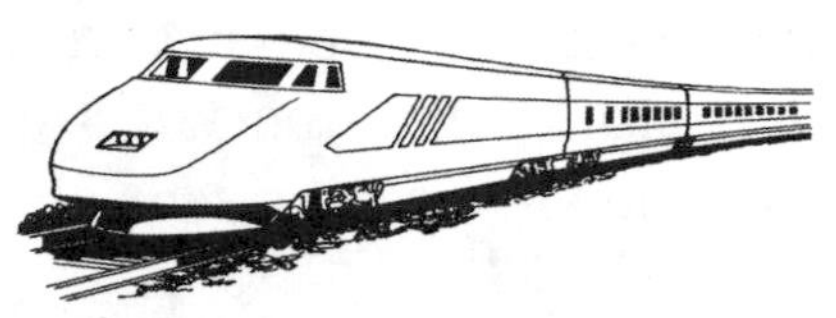

Job opportunity

In 1945, I was a senior in high school in Herington, Kan., a division point on the Rock Island Railroad. During the war years, things were tight and busy, and help was hard to find. Ordinarily, men had to be at least 18 years old to work on the railroad, but the Rock Island Railroad got permission to hire 17-year-olds, which included me.

The railroad people came to the high school, gave their pitch and received several applications. They were looking for brakemen and firemen. After applying and being hired, we were able to make student trips on evenings and weekends. We also had to learn railroading rules and have physical exams.

Most of us were sons of men who were railroaders, and it was exciting for us to follow in our fathers' footsteps. That was especially true for me, since my father was a newly promoted engineer.

It was thrilling to get to work on the railroad. We had

our high-school graduation ceremony the evening of May 17, 1945, and as soon as we got out of our caps and gowns, we went directly to the principal's office to use the phone. We called in and signed up to go to work for the Rock Island Railroad.

My first trip was May 18, 1945. I was called for a Wichita turn, which consisted of doing local work from Herington to Wichita, where we turned the engine around and brought freight back to Herington. What a wonderful experience for a 17-year-old, and I got paid for it, too.

I worked for the Rock Island Railroad for 10 years, and enjoyed every minute of it. I enjoyed each and every experience there. After leaving the railroad, I went back to school and became a pharmacist. Still, I have never really gotten those steel rails out of my blood.

Eddie V. Bales
Mulvane, Kan.

Early day memories

Railroads have been an important part of my life. My hometown was a railroad town. My father, brother, sister, husband, aunt and two uncles all worked for the railroad. Until World War II, railroads employed a lot of people, from call boys to engineers and everything in between.

Trains were our recreation and vacation transportation. Railroad workers and families received free passes to ride the trains. I remember riding "The Dinky" to St. Louis, going to the zoo or to a movie, then riding the rails back home that night.

In the summer, we would ride the train to Arkansas to visit relatives. In the early 1900s, an uncle of mine rode to California by train and kept a diary of the entire trip. Even today, I love to hear a train whistle in the night. The whistles bring back memories of the earlier days.

Muriel Cook
Hurst, Ill.

A thing of the past

In the 1930s and 1940s, I was a child, and my father worked for the Santa Fe Railroad. It was interesting for me, but hard work for the employees. In the summers, I would ride my bike to the shop to take lunch to my father. If, by chance, they were moving a locomotive on the turntable, I got a ride. What fun that was! Those men really worked hard, especially during World War II.

Since my father worked for the railroad, we got free passes. I remember my mother and I taking trips. I'll never forget my first dinner in the dining car – there were finger bowls, beautiful linen and the steward ringing his dinner gong. We knew most of the crew, and a conductor once took me to the baggage car to see dogs being shipped.

Our small town was a division point, and my mother was in charge of the Red Cross canteen next to the station. When troop trains came through, she served them cookies, sandwiches, coffee and milk.

The sounds of the old steam locomotives are a thing of the past, but, oh, how I miss them. Oh, for the good old days.

Betty Bouray
Chanute, Kan.

Thrilling memory of first train ride

Oh, the wonderful memories and heartaches of childhood. I was born to a family in which my father was a boxcar inspector and a wrecker engineer for the Rock Island Railroad in Goodland, Kan.

When I was 4 or 5 years old, I would watch for my dad to come home.

Mom used to say, "Don't you go to the corner to meet your dad."

Well, I always went anyway, but Dad wouldn't let Mom punish me for meeting him.

On warm summer days, my sister and I took lunch to Dad while he was working. It was always a thrill to be close to the trains and sit in Dad's shack and watch as he inspected the boxcars. We would walk on the tracks, looking for old spikes or pieces of coal to take home.

When I was 6 years old, I took my first train ride all the way to Missouri. What a thrill it was to see the porter selling sandwiches, fruit, cookies and candy bars. Mom bought me a candy bar, and I thought I was in heaven for sure.

Heartache came when I was 7 and Dad slipped and fell, breaking three ribs, while inspecting a boxcar. Before his ribs were healed, he got called to a wreck west of town and the wrecker tipped over on him. A man pulled him from the wreckage, but he was never able to work again. After that, I could only sit and watch the trains go by.

But even now, when I hear a passenger train go by, I am still thrilled. I have ridden trains in Germany and all across the United States, but my first train ride holds the most thrilling memory.

Ina B. Smith
Abilene, Kan.

Night track-walker

My father was a railroad night track-walker – an occupation followed by few and found by all to be among the loneliest in the United States. His companions were the moon and stars, the mighty Missouri River and the elements. The worse the weather, the more he was needed to stand at points of vantage and wave his lantern to reassure passing trains on the Missouri-Kansas-Texas (Katy) Railroad that all was clear.

Just like postal workers, my father plodded along in snow or rain, sleet or storm, taking everything in stride, with the exception of hail. In that, he would take cover in one of the many natural shelters in the river bluffs until the worst was over. Part of his job was to watch for rocks or earth that might fall or slide from the bluffs that lined the north side of the tracks where he walked.

He also inspected the track for defects, such as loose connecting bars or broken rails. Along his route, he rarely saw anyone, but he did see wildlife.

That sort of loneliness would drive an average person to distraction, but when he was asked about it, my dad said, "I always did sort of like to go it alone. It's lonely work but not lonesome. Sometimes I go down the track singing, sometimes humming. Ain't got nobody to fuss at me and nobody to fuss at."

The hardest thing for my father was getting used to sleeping during the day. He started work at 7 p.m., and finished at 4 a.m. He would usually get to bed around 5 a.m. and sleep until noon. He worked Tuesday through Saturday, making $242.22 for a 40-hour work week in the 1950s. He walked about 75 miles a week. He drove to work, then got his lantern and signaling equipment from the tool shed and walked down the track about 100 yards to a small shack he used as his base of operations.

My father carried a bag containing three fuses, six

torpedoes and a red flag. He also carried a white lantern and a red one strapped to his back. He walked down the center of the track, shining his light on each side. There wasn't an animal in the country that frightened him – he always walked his route unarmed.

The track my father worked is no longer a railroad track, it's now a bicycle track that runs from St. Charles to Sedalia, Mo.

Mrs. Wilfred Knapheide
Warrenton, Mo.

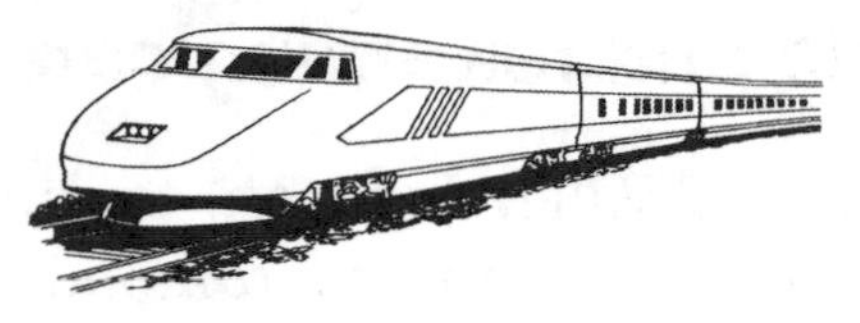

Lesson learned

Although we lived among the beautiful hills of southern Indiana, my dad worked on the railroad in Chicago. Tuesday was his day off, so my mom, my brother and I would commute there via the Baltimore & Ohio each week if he didn't come home.

We often went on Sunday and spent the day having a picnic lunch with him in the tower where he worked as a telegraph operator. We had a wonderful view of the yards, and I was fascinated by the sound of Morse Code. I never understood how Daddy could interpret it so fast.

One Sunday afternoon, my 4-year-old brother and I, 6 years old at the time, were playing among the levers that Daddy pulled to switch tracks in the yard. I vividly remember when we dropped a small, brown pencil among the levers. I also remember how excited they got and how fast Mommy packed up the lunch and took us home. I don't think it caused a wreck on the railroad, but it sure caused my brother and me trouble.

Betty Kavanaugh
Laurel, Neb.

Enjoyable and rewarding career

I was born in Valley Junction, Iowa, now West Des Moines. Valley Junction was a railroad town located at the junction of two railroads in the Raccoon River valley. My father, uncles and grandfather were railroaders.

My father worked in the switchyard as a clerk. His office was about six blocks from our house. Sometimes my brother and I took lunch to him, which entailed walking through the switchyards and the roundhouse. I was 6 or 7 years old at the time, and the walk was awesome and somewhat frightening.

Many of the steam engines would have their boiler fronts removed, being prepared, and I would view them as living beings, with their gaping mouths ready to devour two young boys. As the workers hollered at each other, my imagination ran wild. I envisioned them being devoured by the monster. My older brother gleefully encouraged my thoughts. Eventually I outgrew my fears and traversed the route alone.

Back then, they didn't have a 40-hour work week, no

paid vacation, no paid sick leave and no overtime. Time off was rare. Dad worked from 4 o'clock in the afternoon until midnight every day. This was during the Great Depression, before there were electric lanterns. Dad did his records on a clipboard by the light of a kerosene lantern.

In 1942, I enlisted in the U.S. Army and served until November 1945. During the war, I was trained to be a radio operator, which encouraged me to follow the Morse Code venue into my civilian life. Eventually I became a telegrapher/train-order operator for the Rock Island Railroad.

My contact with other railroaders was enjoyable and rewarding. Many of the trainmen that I delivered orders to were men I had known as a child; they were neighbors and friends of my father. I was proud to be earning top wages, which enabled me to provide a living for my family.

Unfortunately, during my first year as a telegrapher/train-order operator, I was on duty when a horrific crash occurred. I made it through, although I was useless for about 30 minutes when my nerves gave out on me. The accident happened around 6 p.m. and I worked it until my shift ended at midnight. What a dreadful experience.

I eventually wound up working for the railroad in Iowa City, Iowa. It was initially a temporary position but turned into a permanent position. By this time, the unions had negotiated a 40-hour work week, but there was a shortage of telegraphers so I got one day of overtime pay each week. That extra income paid to furnish our first home in Iowa City. After five years in that position, the ticket agent retired, and I moved into his position. I thoroughly enjoyed my job.

In the late 1950s and early 1960s, automobiles and airlines became big competitors, and our passenger business dwindled. Efforts were made by the Union Pacific and other railroads to take over the Rock Island Railroad. I considered leaving but stuck it out hoping the merger would happen soon and my future would look better. When the merger didn't happen, I found employment at a local bank and worked there until my retirement. The last passenger train through Iowa City was in May 1970.

Robert J. Libby
Iowa City, Iowa

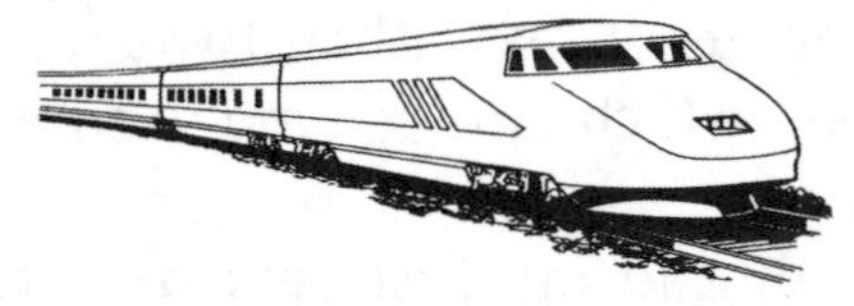

Memories of CB&Q

In 1943, when my husband enlisted, I accepted an assistant agent task in Tarkio, Mo., on the Chicago Burlington & Quincy Railroad. Rationing was in full swing and hard work was in order. I became custodian to a large depot and a billing agent. I also answered phones, collected packages, delivered Killed or Missing In Action telegrams and even learned Morse Code.

My second day on the job, a newspaper story said, "If a feminine voice answers at Western Union, don't hang up, we have a new girl in town." We rented an efficiency room across the street from the school where I had enrolled my 7-year-old daughter.

It was a sad time when I left, but the war was over and the boys returned to their former jobs. Those 34 months were a joy. I'll never forget the friends I made or the cold temperatures.

Glola M. Richardson
Grove, Okla.

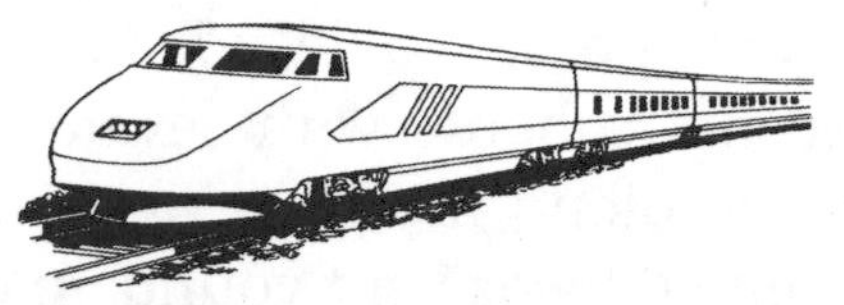

Wailing whistle was comforting

No one who has ever heard it can forget the mournful, wailing whistle of an early 20th century steam engine as it rolls across the American prairie, announcing its arrival at the next town.

In the middle of the night, when there had been a new snowfall, the air was clear as a bell, and the new moon was out in all her glory, the whistle echoed across the plains, drifting into my dreams. Somehow, it was a comforting sound; it had a softness about it. I'd roll over and go right back to sleep, safe under my covers.

My father loved the railroad, loved those big engines. He had worked on the railroad since he was 14 years old. He was hired as a yard boy, which entailed going to railroad employees' houses and giving them a call for their next duty time.

As a child, I didn't see Dad that often. He mostly lived up at the end of his line, in Lusk, Wyo. But when he was home, he would sit with my sister and me by the big, pot-bellied stove telling us fascinating railroad stories.

Dad worked on a spur line out of Chicago called the Chicago North Western. One time, Mama and we kids rode in the caboose. Mama was determined that no matter what, she was going to go to Dad if he could not come to us. We went to the depot and were told that the only train coming through was a freight. He said if she was that eager to go, we could ride in the caboose.

We shared the caboose with several railroad men, and somewhere along the way, we passed through a long, dark tunnel. I was very young, and it really tickled me to go through that dark tunnel. I burst out laughing, which tickled the railroad men, making them laugh too. Mama was just pleased that it hadn't frightened me. We finally reached our destination, and a railroad man took us to Daddy's cabin.

Dad worked on that spur line his whole adult life. One day, he fell out of the cab of the engine and landed on the rails. It bruised his spine, which never healed and turned cancerous.

Kathleen J. Hull
Stockton, Calif.

Family of railroad employees

We were a railroad family, and trains played a large part in my life. My father was a section foreman for the

Pennsylvania Railroad, and my two brothers were wreck derrick operators.

When I was quite young, my father would take me with him on Saturday mornings to run the rails. We would get the old push car out, and Dad would call ahead to get clearance on which way to go first. By doing this, he knew where the trains were and which way they were going.

We watched the rails as we rode, and if we found a broken one, it was marked with a yellow marker. Dad would climb the pole and hook the wire to the telephone he carried with him. Then he would report the findings, and the gang would come out and change the rail.

Several times we went one way, removed the push car from the track and waited until the train went by. I always enjoyed waving to the engineer.

One time, Dad called ahead and was told to stay put until 11 a.m. We waited and waited, and finally, a train whistle blew. Then two more whistles blew.

Dad said, "There's a bad wreck on the west end."

Sure enough, there was the wreck train with both derricks. That whistle had a different sound and you knew what was wrong when they blew the whistle.

Dad phoned again after the train had passed and was told to go back to home base, get his section gang and head west. There were 13 cars, including the engine, off the tracks. In those days, if a refrigerator car was damaged and broken open, whatever was in it was given to the workers and the people in the neighborhood. I can remember Dad bringing home two No. 3

washtubs of dressed chickens. My mother canned them.

To this day, I love to hear a train whistle. I am sure a lot of old-timers remember those days.

Virginia (Holcomb) Steele
Burnettsville, Ind.

Still in touch

The Rock Island Railroad was good to my family. My father worked there and thought that there was no other line as good as his line. He had steady work through the Depression years, and although the wages weren't that great, we managed to get by.

We always had food on the table and clothes on our backs, not to mention the fact that my two siblings and I were able to attend school and get an education. My mother never had to take a job outside the home, so we did all right.

Because of my father's work, we made several moves during my school years. During those moves, I made some very good friends, and to this day, I still keep in touch with them.

The railroad people were given what were called annual passes, and with those passes, we did some train traveling. I love trains! To this day, if I'm not riding, I love to hear them.

Margaret Lewis
Chariton, Iowa

It ain't what it used to be

I come from a railroad family. My mother, aunt, uncle and grandfather all worked for the Santa Fe Railroad. My grandfather was a section foreman who helped lay track from Wichita to Winfield, Kan., at least a hundred years ago. My uncle was a fireman who was bumped during the Depression. He got a temporary job in Cleveland in the Grand Lodge offices of Locomotive Engineers and Firemen, because he could type and take shorthand. He eventually retired from that temporary job.

My mother and aunt worked in the junction during World War I. They had a row of big switches that were operated by hand to keep trains on the proper set of tracks. The Santa Fe Magazine ran a picture of them on duty, which I am lucky enough to have.

I have traveled by train many times. It seems unreal that passenger trains have all but disappeared. We now live in what used to be a very busy rail center on a main line from Chicago to California, with trains going both ways day and night. Now there is one train a day going east and one going west. Both come in the early morning hours. Freight trains go through town all day long, blocking Main Street and frustrating drivers, but if you want to ride on a train, get someone to take you at 2 or 3 o'clock in the morning and go through a station that has been converted to house many businesses. Railroading "ain't what it used to be!"

Christine A. Scott
Newton, Kan.

To Here of Jan 26 - 2002

Chapter 2
War and Trains

Tough times

During World War II, my husband and I managed a hotel where only railroad crews and workmen stayed overnight. Rationing was in full swing, help was scarce, and we had a 1-year-old son and a 6-week-old daughter. At that time, we were not allowed to work our employees more than eight hours a day. However, there was no restriction on the number of hours a manager could work.

Numerous times we were called and notified at the last minute that a passenger train carrying soldiers did not have dinner, and we were expected to feed them. Somehow we managed. I remember one time in particular when I was called and notified at 2 in the morning that there would be 200 soldiers arriving for breakfast at 8 o'clock. There were no stores open, and I didn't have the necessary food coupons anyway. I told the caller we would serve coffee and doughnuts, but not to take any orders for a real breakfast.

I woke my employees, and we began making coffee in 50-pound lard cans and a lot of cake doughnuts. When the train pulled in, the soldiers poured inside and wanted to know where their bacon, sausage and eggs were.

During that time, there was also water on some of the tracks. Train crews were tied up at the hotel until the tracks were repaired. We were unable to send our laundry out, as we were accustomed to, so I ended up washing the sheets in red clay water because they had to be changed daily. Some of the crew decided their sheets had not been changed, so they took clean sheets off the clothesline and put them over the ones already on their beds. Some of them had as many as three layers of sheets to one bed.

Many times I worked 16 hours a day, as well as taking care of my children. At that time, I was learning to drive the company car. Thinking back, I marvel that we managed for several months before giving it up and returning home. I didn't get a medal for my efforts, but I do have the satisfaction of knowing that I did the best I could.

Margaret L. Harris
Tipton, Mo.

Various experiences

During my grade-school years, my mother and I would take train trips to Wichita Falls, Texas, on Friday evenings and return late Sunday. The train we took was the Fort Worth and Denver. This railroad was built before the turn of the century and is still in use.

During World War II, I rode on the Santa Fe from Amarillo to Indian Gap, Pa. What made this trip interesting was that I had to change railroad stations. As I was in a military uniform, I received a good deal of help, telling me how to reach the station.

In a matter of a few days, I found myself on another troop train, bound for Augusta, Ga. When we were in the Washington, D.C., railroad yards, another soldier and I were allowed to get off the train to take trash to an incinerator. Of course, we were really young, and we thought that standing on the grounds of the nation's capitol was a real treat.

Within four months, I was on another troop train going to Seattle. This trip took a full week, because so much time was spent with the train idled because other trains held a higher priority for the use of the tracks. One thing I remember well was crossing Kansas. The state had received a wonderful crop of wheat that year, and those wheat fields looked so beautiful.

Our group didn't stay in Seattle long, and we were told to get ready for another troop train. Eventually, we ended up at the Orlando Air Force Base. A few months rolled by, and I was up for discharge. This time I rode a train to Fort Bliss in El Paso, Texas.

My life has been filled with many wonderful train rides in Canada, Germany and Switzerland. Of course, these train rides were short, but most interesting. The Canadian Pacific gave our party a real treat. We ate in the diner for breakfast, and rode in the glass-top observation coach. Oh, how beautiful western Canada is from an observation coach.

All in all, I know the railroads of the world have had a major part in what we see today in every nation. I, for one, truly love the greatness of the world rail system.

George W. Kendall
Amarillo, Texas

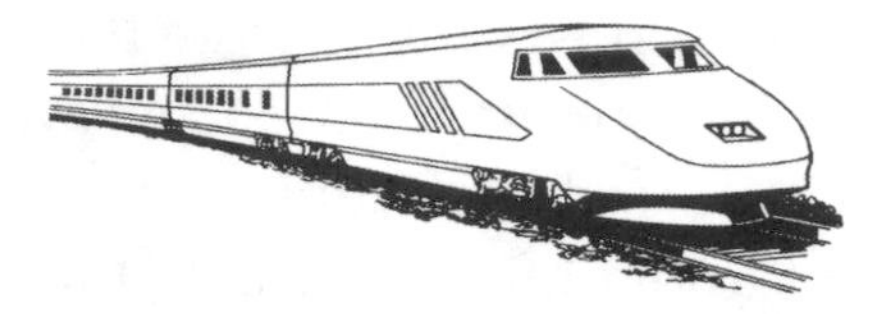

Preferred the bus

I was 11 years old in 1941, when World War II began. The railroads immediately became the means of transportation for the military. It was a daily occurrence to see passenger trains moving in each direction with waving soldiers hanging out of every open window. Freight trains were an equally common sight. Military priority took preference over all civilian travel. It was next to impossible for anyone other than military personnel to travel by rail.

Gas rationing grounded automobiles. Since I was too young to drive, it wasn't an option for me anyway. This, coupled with my need to travel, brought me to the bus. I made many trips between Denver and Buena Vista, Colo.

In 1947, I joined the Navy in Denver, and was given a week to return to Buena Vista, Colo., to settle my affairs before heading to boot camp. They gave me a voucher to catch the train, and when I expressed my preference for the bus, I was informed that the military only used the railroad.

I reluctantly boarded the train for what was to be a very enjoyable and memorable trip. We headed south, making two passenger stops. A swing to the west took us to our next stop. We had just entered the Royal Gorge, when the train stopped and the passengers were allowed to step out and admire the view of the sheer rock canyon and the suspension bridge, 1000 feet above.

The trip resumed, and I have to say, it was the most scenic adventure I've ever had. It was also educational. I learned to close the window in a tunnel. The smoke and cinders have to go somewhere, and if the window is open, they'll go in it. The trip lasted nine hours and was a day well-spent.

I am sorry to say, that experience is no longer available. I didn't realize that trains were passing into history until they were gone.

Ted Knuckey
San Bernardino, Calif.

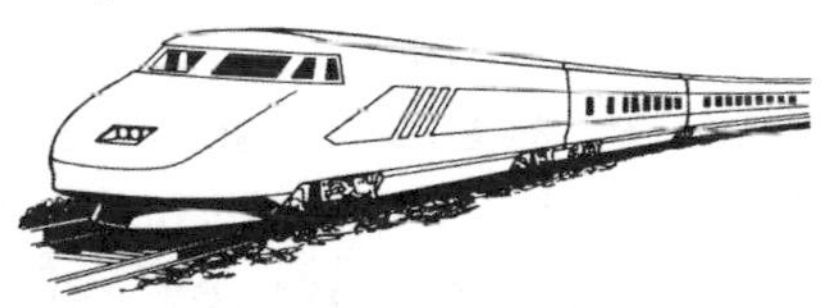

Memorable soldier

When I was 4 years old, my parents took me on my first train trip. We traveled to Oregon to visit relatives.

On the trip home, there were soldiers on the train with us. One nice, young soldier sat in the seat across the aisle. He found a feather, picked it up and blew it across the aisle at me. I picked it up and blew it back at him. We blew that feather back and forth until either the feather was worn out, or we were.

The soldier told me that the duffle bag beside him was filled with feathers. I suppose I believed him. That is one memory that has stayed with me all these years.

Mrs. John McGowin
Jerico Springs, Mo.

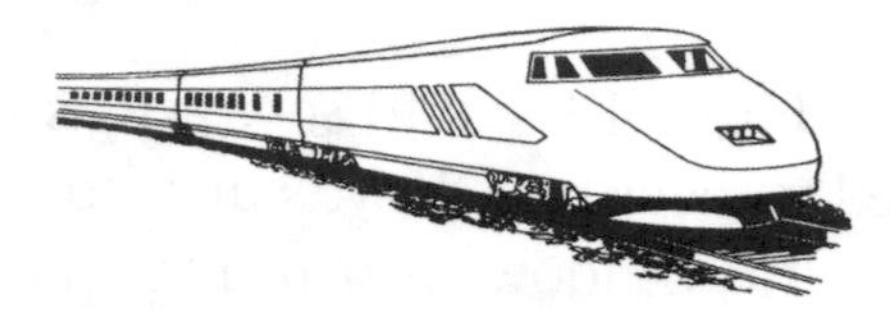

My longest train ride

The longest train ride in my life was when our Air Force unit arrived overseas in 1943. We were loaded on a train in Bombay, India, and transported across the subcontinent to a base near the Burma-India border. We were on three different trains for a total of seven days and nights.

We left Bombay on a standard gauge railway. After a couple of days, we had to unload and reload onto a wide gauge railroad. Finally, after a day or two, we had to detrain and reload on a narrow gauge system. On the narrow gauge, the locomotives and cars are quite small, similar to the type used in mines to carry coal or ore.

The passenger cars on all the trains were equipped with slatted seats that resembled park benches. On the wide gauge, one could stretch out across the bench to rest. On the narrow gauge, this was impossible. The toilet facilities on all trains consisted of a small closet with an eight-inch hole cut in the floor. After reaching our destination, it required nearly two weeks for the men to become rested and regain their physical stamina.

During that time, the train was the only means of transport for the Indian citizens. It was interesting to watch one of their trains from a distance as it moved slowly through the countryside. People filled the cars, and others clung to the outside, wherever they could find a handhold. The roofs of the cars were completely covered with squatting humanity.

There were so many people, the cars were barely visible. Since most of the riders were farmers, when one reached his destination, he climbed down, dropped off and continued by foot. By the time the train reached the next town, only the people seated inside were still on board.

Chet Nelson
Williston, S.C.

Trains were part of career

When I was 8 years old, the first diesel engine pulling one passenger car stopped at our train depot in Oxford, Fla. The principal let the whole school out early, so the children and faculty could go see it. The engine was green trimmed in yellow. The engineer gave us all pamphlets with information about the new diesel engine. He also let us go through it, to see for ourselves what it was like.

The engineer said he would give us a ride to Wildwood, about five miles away, if we could make arrangements to get back to Oxford. I knew I didn't have a way to get back, but I was determined to ride anyway. On the trip, one boy asked me how I was going to get back. I told him I was going to go back with him and his mother, which was news to both of them.

When we got to Wildwood, there happened to be a train headed toward Oxford, so the engineer said we could ride back on it. My parents didn't know anything about it until I got home.

My family eventually moved to Wildwood, the largest railroad center in the southeastern United States of America. Most everybody there worked for the railroad. It was known as The Seaboard Coastline Railway. I remember walking home from school. The train tracks were right beside the highway, and the coal smoker engines blew smoke in my face and cinders would get in my eyes. Sometimes they would let off steam, and I was so scared I would get burned that I would run to the other side of the road.

I went into the service when I was 18. That was in 1945, during World War II. I was inducted into the service and got on one troop train after another and traveled to many different states. These trains were the old coal smokers with no air conditioning, just glass windows with screens.

When the trains went through small towns, people were waiting at the stations to see the soldiers. One kind lady handed me a plate of doughnuts through the window.

While going through New Mexico, our train made short stops in small towns. Young boys got ice cream from the stores and ran alongside the train and the soldiers would hand them money to pay for it.

I was sent to the Philippines on an old Dutch boat that still had the Dutch crew. The war was just over, and about halfway across the Pacific Ocean, they got orders to take the guns down and throw all ammunition overboard.

While stationed in Japan, I had to take a train to the other end of the island where we were stationed to deliver supplies and mail to a soldier at the outpost about 90 miles from the Russian border. I had a whole passenger car all to myself; no one else was allowed in. I stayed with the soldier for a few days in his three-story building, which he had to himself.

I was glad to get on the train to come back to the United States of America for discharge. The train was so long, it took three coal smoker engines to pull it. I had to cook on the train, since I was an Army cook, and we couldn't fill the pots more than half-full or they would spill over. When we got ready to serve the food, we had the soldiers line up and come through the kitchen car, holding their mess kits down beside the pot with the mashed potatoes. We scooped a large spoonful and about that time the train would jerk and the potatoes would land on the floor.

We came to a place out West, where a large pile of rocks had fallen on the tracks. The train crew got mad because the soldiers wouldn't get off the train and help move the rocks. Our commander said that it wasn't our job. We almost ran out of food before we got to the next town, because we sat there for a whole day before the rocks were cleared from the tracks.

In 1949, I decided to make a career of the Army. In 1950, I married the girl of my dreams. We had a son, who now lives in Jacksonville, Fla. I still like trains. In fact, I have a couple of model trains I made from scratch. They are mounted on the wall.

George Likley
Leesburg, Fla.

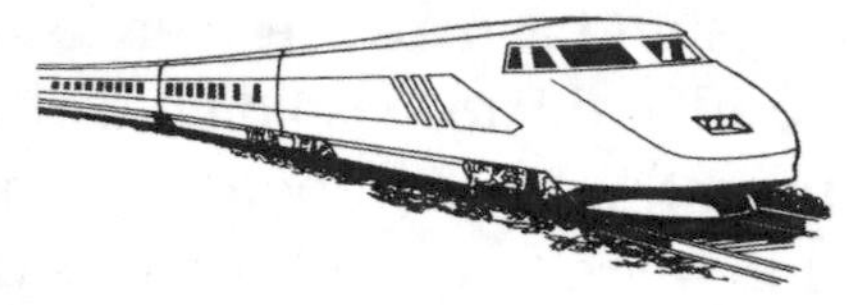

Coming home from the service

I was discharged at Camp Stoneman, Calif., in June 1947. I went to the Santa Fe depot and told them I wanted a ticket to Baring, Mo. We rolled out of the station, and the next thing I knew, we were pulling into La Platt, Mo.

The porter came over to me and told me I would have to get off there, because they didn't stop in Baring, about 40 miles away. But the conductor decided that since my ticket said Baring, that they would stop this time.

So we rolled out again, and pulled into Baring a short time later. Everyone looked shocked to see a private first class getting off the train there. They wanted to know how I got the train to stop there for me.

I simply told them, "That's the service you get when you serve your country!"

James J. Florea

St. Louis, Mo.

GRANGER

Chapter 3
Living by the Tracks

Hanging around the depot

Before the automobile and all-weather roads, the depot was the most exciting place in town. Small towns especially depended upon the railroad for supplies and transportation. The general store not only received all types of supplies, but it used the railroad for shipping cream, eggs and poultry, which had been traded for food, fuel, shoes and clothing.

A popular pastime was to meet the train. It didn't matter whether or not you were expecting anyone to get off the coaches. You could see those city people, with their beautiful clothes, through the window. My best friend's father was the station agent, and he didn't mind us girls hanging around. It was an exciting place, the best in town. We walked up the nice, gravel path to the station, which was clean and freshly painted. The waiting room had long benches, and it was cool in summer. We liked to sit, swinging our feet, listening to the chattering telegraph keys as a message was given in code regarding the train's arrival. It was magic.

As time neared for the train to come, the steel-wheeled hand trucks loaded with freight were pushed out to the side of the track. I can still hear the crunching of the gravel as they were rolled. Empty, flat-bedded carts were ready for the incoming freight, as well as the mail sacks and packages. The moment came when the smoke of the train could be seen in the distance, then the whistling would start. Later, we heard the grinding of brakes and the hissing of steam as it came to a halt.

It was a touch of the outside world and gave one the feeling there was a great and wonderful world out there to see sometime.

Ethel Bruce
Illinois

Raised on the rails

My family once lived in a boxcar for nearly a year. My father worked for the railroad, and he was transferred to a very small town. The railroad company was supposed to have a house built for us when we arrived. Unfortunately, that didn't happen, so my parents, brother, sister and I lived in a boxcar until our house was done. Our boxcar sat on the "right-of-way" beside the tracks.

If we were outside playing when a train came by, we were taught to go back to the fence and hang on until it passed. In the winter, we sometimes woke up with a sifting of snow on our beds, as the boxcar was definitely not airtight.

Before the next winter, we moved into our new house. We all started school, but Dad didn't think we were getting a good enough education, so he asked to be transferred to a larger town, where he became a brakeman on a freight train.

Veda Christen
Waterloo, Iowa

The mill hill cowboys

I grew up on a cotton mill hill, within 50 feet from the railroad tracks. Our family was poor – my father had died when I was only a year old – so my mother worked very hard to support me, my sister, my grandmother and herself. I can remember her making $35 a week.

Rent on our three-room house was deducted from her paycheck. It was based on the number of rooms you had. Our rent was 75 cents a week. Back then, if you missed a day of work, you didn't get paid for it, and yet you still had to pay rent. Out of the 45 years my mother worked, she missed a total of three days.

As a boy, my friends and I were known as mill hill cowboys. We would play on the old steam trains until someone saw us and made us move on. Then we would sit on the banks and watch the trains go by, waving at the passengers on board. It was always a thrill to see the people eating in the club car as they rolled past us.

We just knew they had to be rich.

Living so close to the train station and the roundhouse, where the trains were worked on, we got to see just about everything. We saw both passenger trains and freight trains, including livestock being shipped, which was very common back then.

We often pretended we were train robbers, but unlike Jesse and Frank James, our biggest haul consisted of a few watermelons and some coal, which was intended to help heat our house. The houses back then were extremely cold in the winter and very hot in the summer.

During the World War II years, my friends and I would stand on the banks and wave at the soldiers on the troop trains as they went by. We loved to see the tanks and jeeps being moved. When a troop train stopped, we would run to it and get drinks, candy and cigarettes for the soldiers.

They were always kind to us and threw small amounts of change to us. One time a soldier gave us $3 to mail a letter to his girlfriend back home. For that one day, the mill hill cowboys were rich, and we talked about that man for many years.

As teen-agers, we would sit on the banks and watch as a team of black men put railroad spikes down to hold the tracks together. They sang some of the saddest songs I've ever heard. I became friends with two of the men. Big Paul, who was 6'5" and weighed 275 pounds, and Little Mo, who was 5'8" and weighed about 160 pounds.

I never dreamt that 10 years later, I would become

Paul and Mo's hunting partner. This was something that did not happen in those days – a young white boy riding in the same car as two black men.

Something that was always hard for me to understand was that Paul and Mo worked all their lives for the railroad, yet when we all went down to the train station to rest and get something to eat and drink, they had to eat on one side, while I ate on the other.

I'm glad that before they died, we were able to sit down on the same side, in the train station, and share a sandwich and a Coke together.

The railroad station is long gone. No more trains come by, and the grass has grown up and covered the rails and banks where the mill hill cowboys played. Paul and Mo are gone too. But sometimes I close my eyes, and I hear Big Paul and Little Mo singing as the Silver Star pulls out of Raleigh, N.C.

Richard Dickerson
Raleigh, N.C.

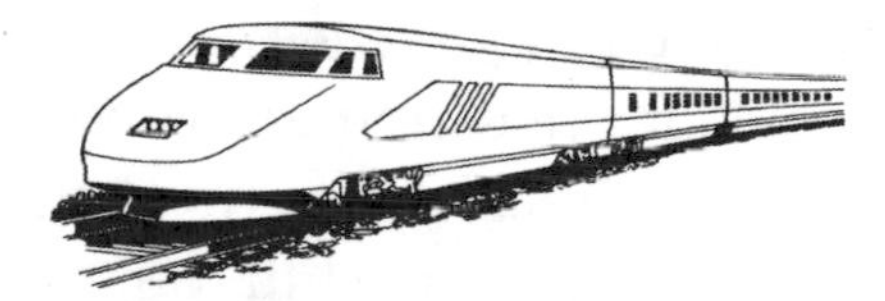

The day our family stopped a train

For 47 years, our family watched the Burlington Northern trains rumble on the rails across 80 acres of farmland, south of our home. To this day, our family has never forgotten the miracle of a freight train, pulling more than 120 cars, that managed to get stopped and prevented a tragedy.

On Memorial Day, 1980, our son, his wife and their three children came to visit us at the farm. That afternoon, my son drove his car along the quarter-mile lane, over the newly graveled railroad crossing so he and his dad could take my grandsons fishing in the big farm pond. They caught three fish, and Grandpa showed them a giant turtle. Then they left the pond to return to the house for supper.

When they drove up the steep slope to go over the railroad crossing, the wheels spun in the loose gravel, and the frame of the car settled down on the iron rails. The car would not move, so my husband decided to get the tractor, knowing that the evening freight train would be coming soon.

My daughter-in-law, granddaughter and I brought the car down to where my son's car was hung up. We heard the train whistle a half mile away, then saw it coming down the track toward us.

My 11-year-old grandson sat down on the ground and cried. My granddaughter leaned out the car window and screamed for her mother, who was unloading what she could from the back seat of the stalled car, while yelling for my son to shut off the motor and abandon the car. My husband's noisy tractor was attempting to pull the car off the track.

Facing the oncoming train, with tears in his eyes, my other grandson stood between the rails doing jumping jacks, yelling "Stop! Stop!" A wise engineer applied the brakes and managed to get the big train stopped, just 30 feet from the car.

The brakeman got out, calmly walked over to us and

said, "No problem, we knew what had happened ... "

We got the car off the tracks, and the big train was on its way again. Our family, however, had lost its appetite, and nobody ate any supper. Today, we all remember that day we were blessed, when our family stopped a freight train.

Frances Forsythe
Albia, Iowa

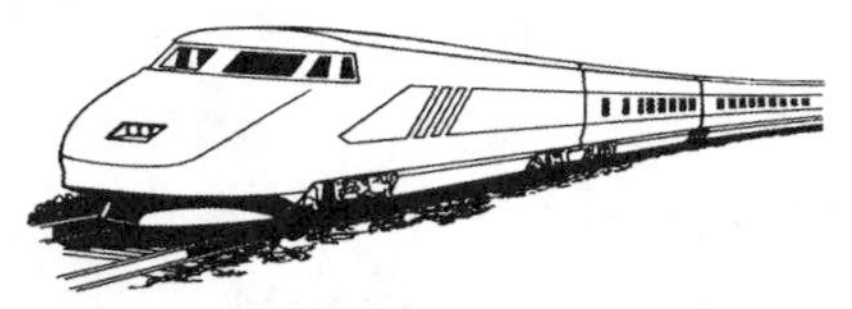

Family was grateful to the railroad

When I was about 12 years old, my father had an emergency appendectomy. In those days, you had to stay in bed for six weeks to recover, so money was very scarce with him not being able to work.

Thank God we lived across the road from the Wabash and Santa Fe Railroads. Since we had no coal to cook with, I would take the coal bucket to the tracks each day to scout for pieces that fell off the trains.

A lot of times, the conductors would see me doing this, and they would throw out a shovelful for me. It was just like black gold. They'd smile and wave at me. They had no idea how grateful my family was for this.

About 3:30 each afternoon, a freight train would stop in front of our house. All the men in our little mining town would get on top of the fruit shipping cars and check to see if they were open. If so, that meant there was ice in them, not fruit. Then the men would pitch the ice out on the ground. The women and kids stood there with tubs to carry it home.

We would put the ice in our iceboxes at the house. Then we could have ice water, iced tea and lemonade. We kids would chip off chunks of it with an ice pick, wrap it in paper and eat it that way. We enjoyed that more than the kids of today enjoy their Popsicles.

Life was hard, but by the grace of God, the trains and the conductors, it got a little bit easier.

Betty Holt
Excelsior Springs, Mo.

The Katy Trail

Most of my life has been spent living on a farm between Matson and Defiance, Mo., which are two small towns about two miles apart. The Missouri, Kansas and Texas Railroad ran through our farm. The lower part was our farmland and the upper part was hills and woods, with the house sitting on a hill.

Our bottom land was along the Missouri river, and we had many floods over the years, which destroyed a lot of crops. The big flood of 1986 washed the tracks out, and it was too expensive to repair them, so the government took them over.

Now the old tracks have become the Katy Trail, which has become very popular with bicycle riders and hikers. Our little towns are now a tourist attraction, especially in the fall, when the leaves are bright and colorful, overlooking the bluffs.

Alma Kamphoefner
Defiance, Mo.

The agent and the berry pickers

It was the turn of the 20th century in the small railroad town of Galt, Ill., when a new agent began working at the depot. The news spread quickly through town. He was young, tall and good-looking. Most important to a particular segment of the population, he was unmarried. His name was John E. Agnew, though most people called him Ed.

Shortly after hearing the news about the new agent, Olive Mae Stacey, a pretty, dark-haired young lady, recruited her little sister for a berry-picking expedition. Their route was along the railroad track that ran in front of the depot. Olive was sure no one would suspect that the prime motivation for the berry-picking excursion was actually to investigate the new agent.

Ed saw the berry pickers in the distance. He casually walked out on the platform, sat down on the bench and nonchalantly began reading a newspaper. As Olive and her sister approached the depot, they saw Ed sitting there reading the paper. What they didn't see was the hole Ed had cut out of the paper so he could observe them without their knowing.

He must have liked what he saw, for he put down the newspaper, strolled over and introduced himself. I'm told that that is how my Grandfather Ed met my Grandmother Olive.

Carol Kosek
Cedar Rapids, Iowa

The "Jerky"

When I was growing up, we lived less than a block – just a small alfalfa field – away from where the "Jerky" stormed through our quiet town twice each day. Those tracks were part of our playground.

We learned early on to "walk seven rails" of track at one time, balancing ourselves without touching a toe to the ground, earning a chance to make a wish. We would place pennies on the rails for the train to flatten, ignoring the warning that such actions might derail the locomotive.

When an approaching train was miles from our local station, we would lie on the ground, amid the wooden ties and the rough, gray gravel, and put our ears on the rail to hear it coming, then laugh at how silly we looked with our blackened cheeks.

We played on the mounds of gravel and sand, which were piled along the siding, telling each other stories we'd heard. We raced down unloading ramps, risking falling, and explored the loading pens in the stockyards, where hobos were said to spend their nights.

When there was a string of boxcars lined up on one of the sidings, waiting to be picked up by the next train, we would crawl to the top of an end car and run across the tops to the other end. Then in the early evenings, we would play inside the cars. Once inside, we would chew mouthfuls of leftover wheat and play "house," while the boys usually played cops-and-robbers.

Fern Ruth
North Newton, Kan.

A day I'll never forget

Trains were a very important part of my early life. At the beginning of the Depression, my family moved from Charleston, W.V., to the country. Steam engines ruled the rails, and the whistle was our clock.

One summer, a work train was doing some ditching and at the time, we lived about 20 feet from the tracks. My brother, Tom, and I were watching everything they did. We didn't notice the engineer walking up behind us until he touched our shoulders. He asked us if we would be interested in catching some crawfish for him to use as fish bait.

Of course we would. We caught about 50 or so from the creek behind our house. Then we put them in a box filled with damp grass. That nice engineer gave each of us a quarter for our efforts. We thought we were rich.

The next day, the engineer told us to climb on and he'd give us a ride. Now this was big time. We probably rode three quarters of a mile, stopped, unloaded a car, then went back. We thanked him, then got off the engine. I will never forget that day.

James R. Kennedy
Leicester, N.C.

Love of trains

When I was growing up, we lived in a little house by the railroad tracks on the Arkansas River. Boxcars filled with chickens, pigs and cattle would park on the tracks and stay there for the night. In the summer, we would sit in our yard and listen to the animals.

Sometimes we would walk to the tracks and try to catch a glimpse of the animals through the rails of the cars. Often we would see hobos hopping into the cars as the train was pulling out. I guess these memories are why I still love trains. I don't even mind waiting at the crossings while a train rolls by. And I still wave at the conductor.

Carolyn Stewart
Collinsville, Okla.

Steam engine train adventures

My love for trains began when I was just a little fellow. We always lived in the country, close to the tracks, while I was growing up. I loved to hear the trains coming up the grade next to our house. It was about a two- or three-mile hill, and boy did those old train engines have to huff and puff to pull all those cars up it. In my mind's eye, I can still hear it.

I remember lying in bed at night and listening to the huffing and puffing. It was an awesome sound to hear in the middle of the night, and a sound I will never forget. The engineer would blow his whistle as they rolled past our house.

During daylight, we would wave to the engineer and anyone else we saw on board as the train went by. There was a sidetrack almost in front of our house where freight trains often pulled over to let fast-moving passenger trains go by.

My brother and I used to go over to the sidetrack when the trains stopped and talk to the engineer. We got to know a lot of them by name. One day when I was about 6 or 7, we walked over to talk to an engineer and he asked us if the blackberries were ripe yet. When we told him they were, he asked if we would pick him about three gallons, so he could take them home for his wife, so she could make blackberry cobbler.

We told him we would, and he told us when he'd be back to pick them up. So, we went to work picking berries. If you've never picked blackberries when it's so hot you can't hardly stand it, let me tell you, it's not a good thing to do. It is a hard job – thorns stick your fingers, you have to be on the lookout for snakes, you get bit by chiggers and you have to be careful of the ticks. But we picked those berries and had them waiting when the engineer came back.

You won't believe what we made per gallon. Would you believe we got 50 cents a gallon for all that hard work? We made $1.50 for that job, or 75 cents each. We thought we were rich. We showed our money to our brothers and sisters and told them what we were going to buy with it at the old country store down the road.

We could hardly wait to go to the store and buy 75 cents worth of candy. We ended up with enough candy to last us two or three weeks. And the next time the engineer came by, he brought our buckets back, and said that his wife had made some of the best blackberry cobbler he had ever eaten. We sold blackberries to the engineers three or four times that summer.

Jonathan Clyde Preas
Lynchburg, Va.

The loud whistle

When my sisters and I were growing up, we lived too far from town to hear a train whistle. One night, our parents took us to visit some friends who lived beside the railroad tracks. We were outside playing, after dark, and we heard a train coming. We raced to climb on a wooden gate closer to the tracks, where we could see better.

The train had one strong light that didn't shine straight ahead like car lights, it swung in semicircles. We smelled the coal smoke and felt the gate vibrating slightly. We knew the engineer in the lighted cab could not see us in the dark, so we were curious when he raised his hand. Suddenly, the whistle blasted so loudly that we almost lost our balance on the gate as we put our hands over our ears.

We screamed and waved our hands as the caboose came into sight, but the engineer couldn't see or hear us. We heard a new sound, though. Our parents were yelling our names. We ran to them, and they hugged us. They thought the train had hit us when we didn't answer them.

Years later, we moved to Queen City, Mo., where Dad began carrying the mail from the post office to the night train. On non-school nights, my sisters and I took turns going to work with Dad. The postal man on the train threw out a sack of mail and grabbed Dad's sack. The train barely stopped moving. I came to the conclusion that the whistle sounds much more lonesome at night.

Our last train experience as children came when our family attended a festival in town. We had ridden to town with our neighbors in their car. They decided they were ready to leave earlier than we were, so our father told them we'd take the train home.

This was during World War II, when gas was rationed and there were a lot of people taking trains. Our train was so crowded that the conductor had us stand in the covered space between the cars. I was a little disappointed that I couldn't see the other passengers, but happy that I got to feel the click-click as the wheels rolled over the cracks in the rails.

Eva Segar
Hamilton, Mo.

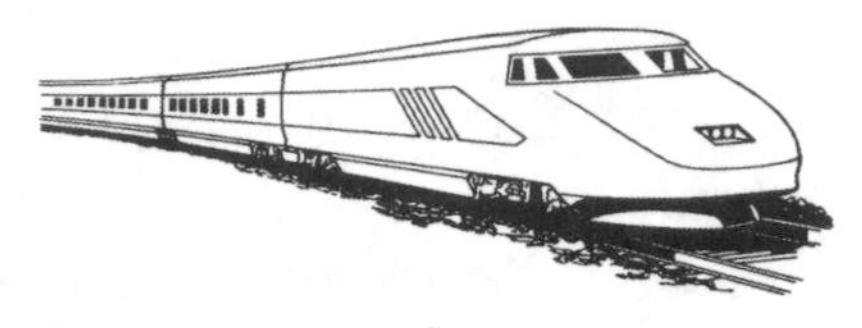

Railroad town

Our town, in southern Minnesota, is a railroad town, built for the Chicago Northwestern Railroad. We miss the passenger trains, which no longer go through town. We could set our clocks by the 3 o'clock train, on its way west.

Our farm was located about a quarter of a mile north of the tracks. We never tired of counting the boxcars, or listening to the rumble and rattle of the lumbering freight heading west. Its piercing whistle at the crossings still echoes in my ears.

My dad was a cattle buyer, and shipped cattle by train. As he rode past, we children would rush out to stand on the big cement block that proclaimed our farm's name. Dad would step out onto the platform on the caboose and wave to us.

My aunt, whose husband worked for the railroad, would come to our house on the passenger train because they had a pass. She would sometimes take me home with her on the train. I thought it was the greatest thrill to hear the conductor say, "All aboard," then come around and collect our tickets. I liked to see him walk down the aisle, grabbing the seats when the train gave a sudden lurch.

The railroad songs that Roy Acuff, Vernon Dahlhart, Jimmy Rodgers and Boxcar Willie sing echo our feelings for the railroad men, who built and worked on the tracks so the Iron Horse could carry people from east to west in our nation.

Lynda Schlomann
St. James, Minn.

Our own playground

I grew up in a very small town in northern Iowa. The farmers put in the Short Railroad line to get their plant and animal products to the market. Six days a week, the train went east in the morning, and west in the afternoon.

In the spring and summer months, the main track and the switch track became our game station. Pump, pump, pullaway and Red light - Green light were only a couple of games we played. Sometimes, in the spring, we would just walk along the tracks and admire the blooming flowers.

As we got older, the tracks made first and third bases for a softball game. The cinders between the tracks were hard on the softball, and on bare feet, if you didn't want to run home to get your shoes.

On Sundays, when the train didn't run, we would push the section car, "Dumpy," onto the tracks. Then we would push it and jump on. We'd have to keep doing this all the way to the bulkhead, where we picked cowslips and looked for Indian heads on a nearby hill.

It was great growing up in a little town. We had so much freedom and our own little playground.

Iona Burlile
Norwalk, Calif.

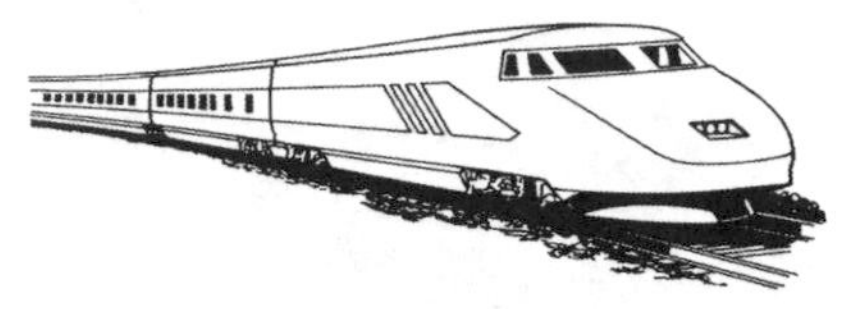

My dream come true

In the summer of 1933, when I was 6 years old, we lived in Woodward, Okla. A spur line of the Katy railroad was just north of our house. The roundhouse, which was where the railroad crew worked on the trains, was about a block west of us.

The switch engineer and his crew, a fireman and a brakeman, walked to work every day. Sometimes I ran up the street and walked back with them. They were my heroes, all because they worked in a Choo Choo.

One morning, the engineer told me if I ever caught him with his steam running, he would take me for a ride, but that his train was currently deader than a door nail. After that day, I constantly checked to see where his train was.

One afternoon, while walking home from school, I saw the engineer's train way up the tracks. I took off running as fast as my legs would carry me. When I reached the front porch, I dropped my books and ran over to a switch where I was sure he would stop at.

When the train got to where I stood, the engineer climbed down from the cab and helped me climb up. Then he sat down in the engineer's seat, picked me up and put me on his lap. He untied his sweat rag and tied it around my neck, put his cap on my head, then told me to pull the cord to ring the bell. Then he told me to pull the other cord, which would blow the whistle. Then he helped me turn a lever and we were rolling down the tracks. I was driving a real Choo Choo. Not many little boys ever got to ride one, and here I was driving one.

We went south about a mile, crossed Main Street, past the depot and went about two more blocks before we stopped in the freight yard. The engineer sat me on the fireman's lap so he could move some boxcars. When he was finished, he climbed back up and we put the train in reverse and backed up all the way to the switch where I had gotten on.

Though it has been more than 60 years since my fabulous experience, I smile every time of think of that engineer and the way he let me think I was really driving that Choo Choo.

Ernest Scharnhorst
Concordia, Mo.

Jan. 28 - 2002
6:30 Evening

Chapter 4
Travel by Train

Small family reunion

In the summer of 1942, my family decided to meet in Idaho, at my sister's house, before my brother left for the Navy. I was living in Nebraska at the time, so my children, ages 3, 4 and 5, and I rode the train.

My husband took us to the train station, which was 13 miles from home, and we began our journey.

We left on a Saturday morning and changed trains in Billings, Mont. After several hours in Montana, we boarded another train and headed for Spokane, Wash. The conductor was very considerate. He had us wait until the servicemen had boarded, then he put us in a car where we each had a seat to ourselves, so the children could sleep through the night.

We arrived in Spokane, Wash., Monday evening and caught the next train to Moscow, Idaho. This trip shouldn't have taken long, but we had to stop for a couple of hours while crews cleared the tracks where there had been a train wreck.

We finally arrived in Moscow, Idaho, about 2 a.m. There was nobody there to pick us up. A taxi driver asked if we needed a ride, but I explained that my family was picking us up. He left to take someone else somewhere and returned to find us still sitting there. He asked me again if we needed a ride. This time I gladly accepted. He took us to my sister's house, and we woke everybody up.

The reason nobody was there to meet us, was because I had sent a letter, expecting them to get it on Monday, not realizing that there was no mail delivery on Labor Day. To make matters worse, our luggage did not arrive when we did. I had packed an extra outfit for each child to put on the train with me and checked the rest. We stayed for 10 days, and our luggage showed up the day before we left.

Mrs. Leland Aspegren
Oklahoma City, Okla.

When the trains ran

My son returned from a trip on Amtrak and told of incredible sights of Western mountain passes and valleys. He spoke of gourmet meals as the train sped through California.

I have trouble reconciling this experience with what I see around me. The tracks that hummed during my childhood are overgrown with weeds or have been transformed into hiking trails. The railroad station in Marion, Iowa, where a school friend joined me on our trip to college, is now the centerpiece of Marion's park, and it is used as a community center. How many old depots are now restaurants or shopping malls?

I also have trouble reconciling my son's experience with the trains of my youth. They were meant to carry freight and people, often in that order, and no one expected extras. They were dependable, and they took us places we would never have seen without them. They were noisy with their clickety-clack over the rails, ringing crashes as cars coupled, and long, mournful whistles that echoed over the fields. They were often sooty with coal dust that blew in through open doors and windows from the coal hopper, but despite their noise, dirt and general discomfort, we didn't complain. Trains were our lifeline to the world.

If it had not been for the Hiawatha that streamed through Iowa into Chicago, I probably would have gone to school, married and lived all my life within 50 miles of my childhood home. Because of the train, I went away to college in September 1947, and I have lived in a city ever since. I got on the train in a small Iowa town, and after five hours, got off in the heart of Chicago, on Michigan Avenue.

On the trip to college, my best friend and I had five suitcases between us. They had been no problem on the train, when we had the aid of a porter. Getting them onto a crowded bus was quite a different story. We had to transfer three times.

On later trips to the city, we had a unique way of signaling the train. The Hiawatha ran through our farm, and my stepfather would go to the field nearest the track and wave a kitchen towel. Then he scurried back to the car and drove me to the station. There was the train, waiting for me, a smiling porter on the steps, ready to give me a hand.

Upon my return at the end of college, having collected a few possessions along the way, I now had a small trunk of belongings. It had been picked up for me and was coming on a later train. When the stationmaster called and announced that my trunk had arrived, I asked when it could be delivered. I saw my stepfather bend over in amusement and embarrassment. Of course, no one expected such personal treatment in rural Iowa. I was sharply reminded that I was no longer a city girl.

Donna M. Cole
Cedar Rapids, Iowa

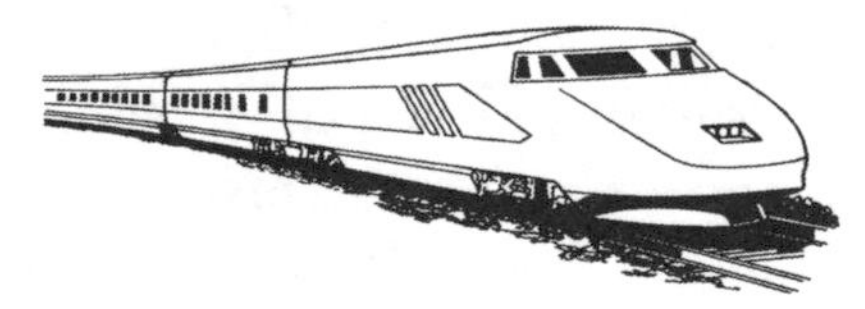

Many memories

I vividly remember my first train trip. I was 16 years old, living in a small farm town in Iowa, when my sister and I took the train to visit our relatives in Kansas City, Mo. We took the Interurban, an electric train, from our hometown to Des Moines, Iowa. From there we rode the Streamliner to Omaha, Neb., where we had to taxi between stations in order to get our connection to Kansas City.

My much older, married sister was very nervous, and sure that we would get lost in Omaha. I remember feeling like an adult as I took charge of everything. I made sure we had our luggage, I hailed the taxi and made sure we arrived at the correct gates. My sister just kept asking if I was sure we were at the right place, and was I sure I knew what I was doing. Of course, I wasn't sure, but I put on a big front, and we did arrive safely in Kansas City, Mo.

Later, while I was in nurses training, I rode the train between Rochester, Minn., and home whenever I could get a weekend leave.

A few years later, I married a handsome, young man who became a railroad fireman and later, an engineer. He had no regular run, but instead worked off of the extra board. He had to leave for work on short notice, which caused him to miss several family events.

My favorite memory of my many train trips occurred while my husband was working early one morning. He stopped at our home, in a small Minnesota town, about 3:00 o'clock, and persuaded me to ride to Minneapolis in the engine with him. That was a no-no, but who would know at night? So I went, and we drove home in the car he kept at the Minneapolis depot, arriving home in time to get the kids up for school.

Since that time, we have ridden on trains in Scotland, England, Norway, Sweden, China and Russia. The Norway trip was memorable for my husband because the engineer let him ride in the cab, as a courtesy to an old railroader. Our trip from Edinburgh, Scotland, to London was exciting, too. We had to stop to allow herders to get their sheep off the tracks.

I fell in love with trains during World War II, and that

love affair has continued during the years. Now we are looking forward to riding the train in Germany and France and through the Chunnel under the channel to visit friends in England.

Maxine Ernst
Minneapolis, Minn.

A dream come true

For many years, my husband dreamed of him and I taking a train trip together. We finally did, when we were both past the age of 60. The trip was supposed to take two days and nights. We decided to go the most economical way, and take our own food. Our daughter prepared sandwiches for us and put them in the freezer so they would keep until we left. Of course, when we left, we forgot them. Luckily, we had remembered apples and crackers.

Riding through the countryside, we witnessed delightful views of Midwest farms and pretty back yards in small towns. The tracks ran through the busy part of Old Chicago, and we were glad for scheduled stops, allowing passengers to depart the train and take invigorating walks up and down depot areas.

In the early morning sunshine, we rode in the observation car, which had a glass ceiling and walls. While crossing through Wyoming, the conductor pointed out buffalo and antelope.

The dining car was as beautiful as the pictures we'd seen in our schoolbooks years ago. The tables were covered with fresh, white tablecloths, napkins, polished flatware and flowers. A handsomely uniformed gentleman, with a white towel draped over his arm, took our order. The food was as tasty as what we would have prepared at home.

Eventually we reached the station and were thankful to our friend, who had left his bed to meet us at 5 o'clock in the morning.

When asked if we would take another train trip, our answer is "Yes, I think we would. Only the next time, we'll be sure and remember the sandwiches."

Elaine Carr
Nyssa, Ore.

Leisurely journey

Some of the happiest recollections of my childhood are the train trips I took. I grew up in a small railroad town during the Depression years. In those days, things were quite different; cars were definitely a luxury item, and not many people owned them. We walked everywhere we went.

There was one passenger train that came through town at 7:30 a.m. en route to Indianapolis and returned at 7:30 in the evening. During that time, the railroad issued free passes to their employees, entitling them and their families to ride their trains. So we occasionally went to Indianapolis for the day.

What a treat that was! My mother, brother and I would get up early, eat breakfast and walk the six or seven blocks to the train station. If we were a little early, we would go and sit in the waiting room, which had an atmosphere all its own. Wooden seats with fancy wrought iron dividers defined each person's allotted space.

The telegraph operator had his own little cage where he tapped and received mysterious and important messages. From time to time, he would report the arrival and departure of trains. He also doubled as a ticket agent.

At last, we would hear the whistle of our train and rush out to see it steaming grandly down the track, bell ringing, whistle blowing and the headlight shining like a giant yellow eye. The train crew always waved; they seemed to have a special place in their hearts for children. The conductor would call, "All aboard," and we would climb the magic steps into another world.

The train consisted of the steam engine, one mail car and one passenger car. The seats were covered in a beautiful, bright-green plush material with white linen-like covers on the head rests. The backs of the seats could be pushed forward or backward, so that one or two of us could ride backwards while facing Mother, who preferred riding forward.

At last, the wheels would begin to slowly turn, and before we knew it, we would be crossing the Wabash River. It was a leisurely journey as we stopped at every little town along the way, but we enjoyed every minute of it. The high spots of the trip were when we crossed the Tulip Viaduct and went through the tunnel.

All too soon, the conductor would announce Union Station, and we would marvel at all the trains as we made our way out into the city. Before we knew it, it was time to return home. By the journey's end, we were all ready for supper and bed, but very happy we had gone.

Eleanor Goodwin
West Salem, Ill.

My family and trains

Throughout my childhood, I traveled by train from Port Allegany to Williamsport, Pa., which was more than 100 miles. Twice a year, my mom, sisters and I took that trip to visit Grandma and Grandpa. We would go for two weeks around Christmas and two weeks in the summer.

When I was about 8, I asked one of the train men what they did in the mail car and baggage car. I got permission to go back to the baggage car and observe the men doing their jobs. To this day, my oldest sister is jealous because I got to go and she didn't. She was told by the train man that only boys were allowed in the baggage car.

As we went through a little town called Driftwood,

the train slowed down, a man opened the door and threw out a couple of mail bags onto a baggage cart that sat beside the track. The engineer knew if they needed to stop, as he had a stick with a wire loop that he held out the window to snatch the train orders from the telegrapher at each section. The conductor let the engineer know when the train was ready to move, by pulling on a cord in the passenger car, which sent a signal that the train was ready to proceed.

One thing we kids thought was neat was going around sharp curves. As we did, we could look out the window and see the engine and the rear of the train at the same time.

Grandma and Grandpa lived right across the tracks from the railroad station, so Grandpa would meet us at the station, and Grandma waved from their back porch.

In those days, Christmas season on the train was a special treat. The train was always crowded with servicemen and others who were headed home for the holidays. One year it was so crowded that people were standing in the aisles because all the seats were taken. Mom put our suitcase on the floor and my sisters sat on it until we got to Renova, where some more passenger cars were added.

During World War II, many soldiers who had lost their lives in the war were being returned home for proper burials. Mom's cousin was an escort for the Army, and it was his job to stay with the remains until he was returned to his loved ones. I always looked for our cousin when the baggage door opened.

When I graduated from high school, I went to Williamsport to look for work. I was really interested in working for the Pennsylvania Railroad, but first I got a job working in the train station concession stand. Every day after work, I went to the trainmaster's office and bugged him for a job on the railroad.

One day, when I got to his office, he gave me an application and told me he had a job available on the track crew. I was hired and sent to Newark, N.Y., which was a little spur line on a coal route.

When the trains jumped the tracks and tore up the railroad, the crew I worked with would get overtime to repair the track so the trains could move again. I only worked a short time on the five-man crew, as this was about the time the railroad was doing away with the section gangs and replacing them with special work trains.

William H. Grandin
Roulette, Pa.

Means of transportation

In 1940, while teaching in a country school, I had no car, so I had to travel to the teachers' meetings by train. Later that year, I promised four of my students a train ride if they earned a State Reading Circle certificate. All four of them earned their first train ride ever. It was just a short ride, about 20 minutes long, but they loved it.

Trains have been an important part of my life. Many times, the train has been my only means of transportation.

Mary E. Stockstill
Waynesville, Mo.

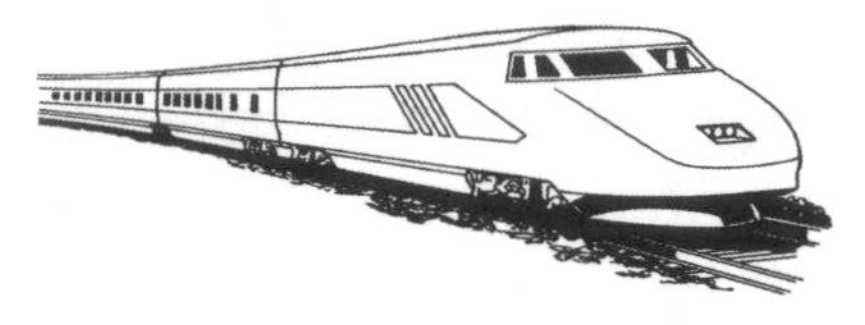

Lost treasure

Trains were an important part of the economy of my southern Ohio hometown. Many people were employed by the train lines, including my neighbor. He made me a wonderful lamp out of part of an engine.

More than watching the trains, was the thrill of riding one. My mother, a good friend, her daughter and I made several trips to West Virginia. What a thrill it was for two preschool girls.

Another special memory for me was when Dwight D. Eisenhower was campaigning for president. His train made a stop in our area, and we were dismissed from school to go see him. How wonderful, that a train could bring a piece of history to us.

Trains became very important to me when I was in high school. My boyfriend lived more than 100 miles away, but his dad was an engineer, so he got free passes to visit me. Later, my class took the train from Ohio to Washington, D.C., and New York City on our senior trip. We had a marvelous time on the train, though I'm not sure the other passengers did.

When I attended college and wanted to go home, I took the train. The trip lasted about three hours, which gave me time to study, relax or dream about my future. Later I took some short excursion train trips, just for sightseeing. One of them included a wonderful meal with fancy tablecloths, candlelight and flowers.

It's been awhile since I've climbed aboard a train, but hardly a day goes by that I don't hear a train whistle coming from the tracks a couple of miles from my home. My attachment to trains goes back to my early childhood, when I stood in the back yard and watched the trains go by every day. I love trains! Now that I'm retired, maybe I'll become a hobo and ride the rails!

Joyce A. Munn
Watts, Okla.

Part of my life

During World War II, my sister and I worked in Chicago at a defense factory that made walkie-talkies for the service. We lived on a farm 200 miles south of Chicago.

The Illinois Central Railroad had a passenger train that left the South Chicago station each night and went through our hometown. Once or twice a month, on Friday night, we rode the train home. It stopped in every town, big or small, to pick up or let off passengers. If we were lucky, we each got a seat to ourselves.

We would stop in Champaign, Ill., and the conductor would get off and have breakfast. While we waited, vendors would get on the train to sell coffee, milk, doughnuts and wonderful ham sandwiches. It was 8:30 a.m. by the time we finally got to our hometown. Then we had a mile walk to our parents' house.

I have good memories of our train trips home. Now, the trains go a lot faster and make fewer stops. My grandfather and my uncle both worked for the railroad, which will always be a part of my life.

Lavona Jones
Edgewood, Ill.

Frightened

When my husband was in the Army Air Corps, in 1943, I left my two small children with my parents and set out for Tennessee. I boarded a steam train in Oakland, Calif., and was to ride to Nashville, then take a bus to Cookeville, Tenn.

I wasn't too thrilled to be on a train going up into the Sierras, but after a few hours, I was completely unnerved by the crashing and banging sounds of a train. I asked a conductor what all the noise was, and he said, that in order for the train to make it over the mountains, it was necessary to hook on a couple more engines, and that was what the racket was.

I wasn't completely convinced. I was sure we were

going to go over an embankment, or some other dire fate would befall us. At that point, the conductor told me, "You are as safe as if you were in God's pocket." I often think of that kind man who was so reassuring to a 25-year-old fraidy cat. I was a city gal at that time and had never been on a train in my life.

Dorothy L. Odetto
Novato, Calif.

The last train out

For several weeks in 1971, the Independent Record, the daily newspaper in Helena, Mont., hinted at the demise of the Burlington Northern Railroad passenger service into and out of the town. The focus of the railroad company's problem stemmed from diminishing passenger usage.

For years I had conveniently used the rails for round-trip transportation from Billings to Helena and back. I had enjoyed riding the train to visit family and friends. But now I lived in Helena with my husband and our 8-year-old son, and there wasn't a need for me to ride the train.

While reading about the plight of the Burlington Northern one morning over a cup of coffee, it dawned on me that my son had never ridden a train. He'd never experienced the clickety-clackity bumps as the cars swayed almost rhythmically behind the huge, gleaming steam engine as it picked up speed on the flats.

He'd never heard firsthand, the shrill whistle at crossroads, and he'd never enjoyed the announcement of dinner by the tinkling of a silver bell as the porter walked through the cars.

When the final days of the passenger train became imminent, I took action. After discussing my plan with my husband, we agreed that our son and I would ride the last scheduled passenger train out of Helena. My husband would meet us with the van at a planned destination and take us back to Helena.

April 24, 1971, was a beautiful spring day. I remember the smell of lilacs in the air and the sun shining warmly as we stepped up to the window to purchase our tickets.

"That will be $1.25," said the man behind the window.

My son handed him the money.

The ticket agent stamped a few pieces of paper, then, very officially, handed Joey his ticket and said, "Hang on to this one, son. It's a collector's item."

We hurried outside to the platform and found a porter waiting with a metal stepstool for us to use to climb up steep steps and into the waiting car. We had barely found our seats when we heard, "all aboard," and felt the train jerk beneath us. With a long pull on the whistle, the engineer slowly glided out of the station.

Happily, I watched my son point to unexpected surprises outside the window. One surprise was a herd of antelope that grazed alongside the tracks.

I remembered my own happy times spent riding the train home to visit family and friends for Christmas and Easter holidays during the late 1950s and '60s. The flexibility of riding the train had given me peace of mind during uncertain weather, typical of seasons in Big Sky country. And I met interesting people on the road to their own adventures.

Lenore McKelvey Puhek
Helena, Mont.

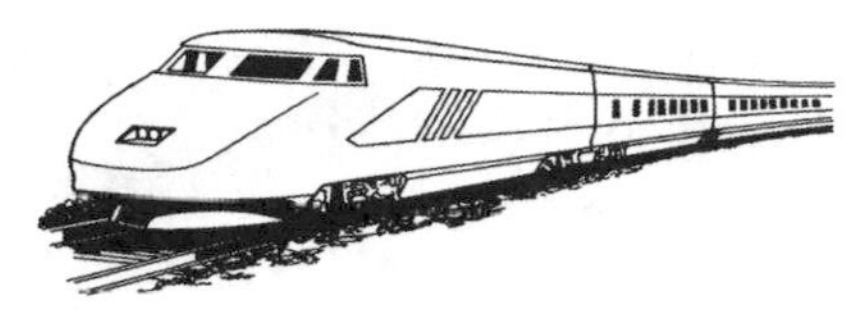

Refreshing

When I was growing up in Iowa, each of the small towns we went to for marketing had train tracks crossing one edge. I got used to watching the trains go by, as we sat waiting for a clear road ahead.

At night, I snuggled down in bed and listened to the mournful sound of the whistle echoing across the cold, still Iowa plains. Later, when I went to work in California, that same train took me home on vacations and in the summer.

One spring, a light rain shrouded Los Angeles' Union Station as I walked across wet asphalt toward the building. I stopped just inside, my bleak mood interrupted by the impact the place had. The vaulted ceiling lifted my senses and expanded my feelings, pulling me toward the train tracks.

Trains on tracks, the hustle of loading, steam, people

and "all aboard," kept the June gloom at bay. I found my place, arranged my things and settled back, watching the rain sweep across the tracks, my mind adrift. Then the train eased out, and with its motion, I slept.

All the way across the Western states, I alternately dozed, then roused to watch the moving countryside.

Needless to say, I arrived in Omaha, Neb., refreshed and invigorated. Mother met me in the station. I could not wait to get home and reach the shelter of the woods, to sit beneath the oak trees and watch the water burbling over the stones of the brook, on its way to the river. All of this was possible for me because of that great train ride!

Barbara Queen
Rosemead, Calif.

Beautiful view

I was born in Oregon, but my parents brought me at a very young age to live in Missouri. We came by train, but I was too young to remember. My mother often told me about the beautiful mountains, and the train that went by our home in Oregon. I always wanted to see it for myself. Then one day, my chance came.

I was about 50 years old when my sister and I decided to take a train trip to see my daughter, who lived in Oregon at the time. We spent a lot of time in the Dome car, so we could see the country and towns as we rode along from Kansas City, Mo., to Hood River, Ore.

We had a wonderful time. I could lay in bed at night and hear the train whistle as I drifted off to sleep. What a thrill it was to stand there and view the early history of my life. The train trip home was good too. We ate in the dining car and met a lot of people.

Velma Smith
El Dorado Springs, Mo.

Hopeful

As a young child, living in a small Kansas town, my life was good. Then my father took a job with the Ford factory in Flint, Mich. After school let out for the summer, my mama, two sisters and I boarded the train in our small town and headed to Michigan for the summer. The trip took several days and nights. I remember eating oatmeal in the dining car and going over a huge bridge one night. It was an impressive first train ride!

Later, as a young woman, I became friends with another young woman who lived in my duplex. Her husband worked for the railroad and was away quite often. Eventually, they were transferred to San Antonio, Texas, and I missed her very much.

I decided to visit her, and wound up on a train headed for Texas. The train was packed with servicemen. It was a long, hot trip, with the cinders coming in through the open windows, but I truly enjoyed San Antonio and the time I spent with my friend.

During World War II, I took a train to meet my future husband, who was coming home on a 30-day leave from the Navy. We had been engaged for a year, and during his leave, we were married. What an exciting train ride that was.

I am now living in Wichita, Kan., and I hope that Amtrak will come through our town. I would love to ride the rails again!

Virginia M. Moss
Wichita, Kan.

Lifetime pass

When I was 10 years old, we had a visitor from "far away." We knew cousin Sadie from her letters, but we never dreamed of getting to know her in person. One winter, she wrote us that she was planning to pay us a visit.

When her husband retired from the railroad, where he had held a position of authority, he was given a lifetime pass for him and Sadie. Determined to take advantage of the pass, Sadie decided to travel to Indiana and get acquainted with her cousins.

I knew she lived in Marshalltown, Iowa, but that had always seemed like the other side of the world to me. The farthest I had been from home was the county seat, which was only 15 miles away!

along from Kansas City, Mo., to Hood River, Ore.

We had a wonderful time. I could lay in bed at night and hear the train whistle as I drifted off to sleep. What a thrill it was to stand there and view the early history of my life. The train trip home was good too. We ate in the dining car and met a lot of people.

Velma Smith

El Dorado Springs, Mo.

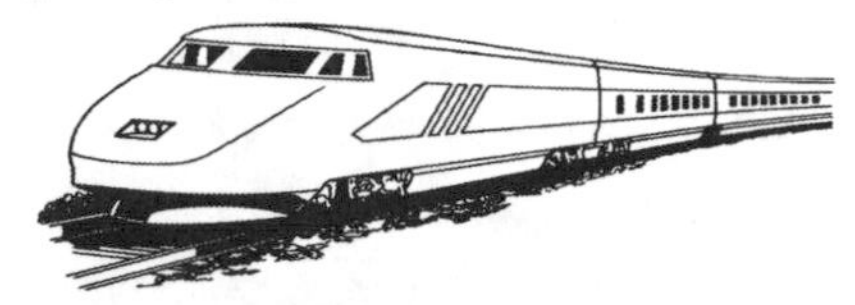

Hopeful

As a young child, living in a small Kansas town, my life was good. Then my father took a job with the Ford factory in Flint, Mich. After school let out for the summer, my mama, two sisters and I boarded the train in our small town and headed to Michigan for the summer. The trip took several days and nights. I remember eating oatmeal in the dining car and going over a huge bridge one night. It was an impressive first train ride!

Later, as a young woman, I became friends with another young woman who lived in my duplex. Her husband worked for the railroad and was away quite often. Eventually, they were transferred to San Antonio, Texas, and I missed her very much.

I decided to visit her, and wound up on a train headed for Texas. The train was packed with servicemen. It was a long, hot trip, with the cinders coming in through the open windows, but I truly enjoyed San Antonio and the time I spent with my friend.

During World War II, I took a train to meet my future husband, who was coming home on a 30-day leave from the Navy. We had been engaged for a year, and during his leave, we were married. What an exciting train ride that was.

I am now living in Wichita, Kan., and I hope that Amtrak will come through our town. I would love to ride the rails again!

Virginia M. Moss
Wichita, Kan.

Lifetime pass

When I was 10 years old, we had a visitor from "far away." We knew cousin Sadie from her letters, but we never dreamed of getting to know her in person. One winter, she wrote us that she was planning to pay us a visit.

When her husband retired from the railroad, where he had held a position of authority, he was given a lifetime pass for him and Sadie. Determined to take advantage of the pass, Sadie decided to travel to Indiana and get acquainted with her cousins.

I knew she lived in Marshalltown, Iowa, but that had always seemed like the other side of the world to me. The farthest I had been from home was the county seat, which was only 15 miles away!

What an exciting day it was when she finally arrived on the train, with her suitcase and a big hug for everyone. She was such a sweet, friendly person, and her visit brought great pleasure to all of us – thanks to the train.

Alma Smock
Monrovia, Ind.

The old trains

My grandfather worked in the coal chute for the railroad, so my mother and her family would often ride the train. They, of course, received free passes because of my grandfather's employment. Then the coal chute shut down, engines took the place of coal, and the job ended.

My father-in-law rode the train a lot. He brought lumber, nails, posts, barbed wire and supplies from Iowa to Colorado, and built the homestead house that I now live in. He would also put their cattle, hogs, cream and eggs on the railroad cars to be sold in Denver, which was more than 100 miles away.

I remember as a child, my dad held me up so I could see President Roosevelt sitting on the caboose of a train that passed through our hometown of La Salle, Colo. He was the only president I ever got to see.

I think the old trains were beautiful, with the smoke from the smoke stack, the horn and the cattle guard on the front end. They win hands down over the newer trains. I rode a train to Denver once to get state aid after my husband had a farming accident that took his leg. We received our aid, and my husband was able to receive his wooden leg. He took each of our six children with him to Denver by train when he went to the doctor.

Later, my husband and I took a ride on one of the oldest trains and had a wonderful vacation. Nothing can replace what trains have done and are still doing for the good of everyone.

Bettie Sampson
Akron, Colo.

Train ride to the state fair

As a teen-ager in the late 1940s, I was at our county fair when a man I knew approached me and asked me to accompany him to the State Fair in Pueblo, Colo., to help him show cattle. I lived in eastern Kansas and had never been to Colorado. My eyes lit up, and I was ready to go.

One night in late August, we loaded 18 head of Ayrshire dairy cattle into the bottom of a double-deck sheep car and headed out on the Atchison, Topeka & Santa Fe Railroad. The top deck was raised to accommodate the cattle, with their feed, water, straw, etc. We crawled around in the top half. My employer had a cot he slept on, but I was forced to sleep – or should I say, try to sleep – on the feed sacks. It got very chilly at night, too, and all I had was my suitcase and no blanket.

Our cattle car had open slats for ventilation and we were placed right behind the steam engine, since that was supposed to be the smoothest place in the line of cars. The black smoke came back into the car along with steam and the cold night air. All that combined with the clickety-clack of the tracks, the swaying of the train, the blowing of the whistle at each cross road and the speeding up and slowing down made a very uncomfortable ride.

The next morning, we pulled into a freight yard, where I found out that part of my job was to milk three cows. I started milking but the car kept moving around, as it was switched to another train. Suddenly, our car apparently got bumped by another string of cars, and the cows fell over sideways, like a bunch of dominoes, with me in the middle milking.

After things settled down, and we fed and watered the cows, the train crew stopped and asked if we wanted a ride to breakfast. So we hopped into the big steam engine and proceeded down the tracks to a small cafe. Inside, I was encouraged to order a stack. I had never heard the term before, but that's what I ordered – every morning for the rest of the trip. Those sure were good pancakes in that nice, warm place. Especially after the night I had spent. They cost $1. I had agreed to work for $3 a day, so I couldn't spend over $1 a meal.

After boarding the cattle car again, I found we had a small tub of pop bottles, but the ice had melted. I was told to look for a refrigerator car, also know as a reefer. In each end of a reefer, there was a big ice compartment, with a door in the top where they put the ice in. Whenever the train would stop, I would look for a reefer and run up the ladder looking for ice, trying to hurry so I wouldn't get left behind.

Here was all that pop, which I dearly loved, but I couldn't throw out the milk, so I cooled the milk and drank it instead. At one stopping point, I spotted some children playing, so I yelled at them to bring some containers and I would give them some milk. With some of the milk out of the way, I could drink pop for a little while.

We were on a local train, making stops all along the way. At one stop, in the middle of nowhere it seemed, we found that one of the cars had a hotbox. It was smoking, and we, along with the train crew, stood in the hot sun sprinkling water on the axle to cool it down.

After several hours, I proceeded to the caboose, climbed up in a nice seat and thought I'd ride in style. However, the conductor soon came along and chewed me out. I guess he thought I might send some false signals to the engineer.

By this time, we were running behind schedule, and my boss began complaining. Shortly afterward, our car was put on a Red Ball train, which didn't stop for anything, and we sped toward Pueblo for the state fair. We rode back the same way, stopping and showing cattle at two more fairs along the way. By the time I got home, I was black from smoke and dirt, with about the same amount of money in my pocket as when I left. I made $3 a day and spent $3 a day on food and the races and rodeos. I still love trains, especially the steam engines.

Charlie Wagner
Atchison, Kan.

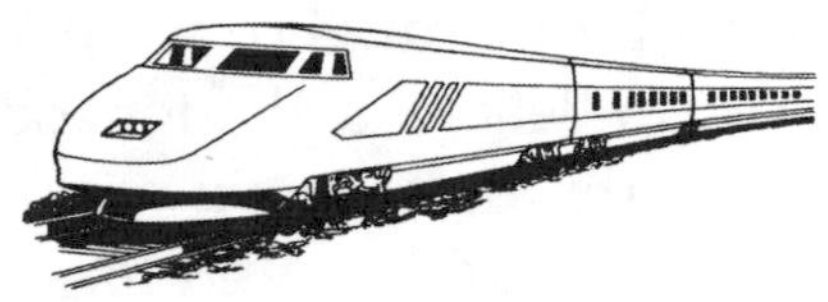

The magic of trains

From the time I was a child, I felt the mournful sound of a train whistle in the night, calling me into the unknown. I had a secret dream.

I traveled the rails at an early age, because my dad commuted from New Jersey to New York City, and he sometimes took me with him. At that time, two railroad lines went to the city. The Pennsylvania went under the Hudson River directly to New York. The Jersey Central stopped on the New Jersey side of the river and discharged all its passengers, who then had to take a ferry. The ferry ride was the icing on the cake. One time, Daddy let me choose which train we would ride. Not realizing there was a difference, I chose the Pennsylvania and almost cried when I figured out we didn't get to ride the ferry.

In July 1951, at the age of 18, I enlisted in the U.S. Air Force, and took off for basic training in San Antonio, Texas, not on a plane, but by train. It was my first time away from home. The other girls and I boarded amid bells, whistles and shouts of "All aboard."

We chugged out of the station, barely able to contain our excitement, and began to get acquainted. Dinnertime came, and armed with government vouchers, we settled ourselves in the dining car. After ordering from the menu, we stared, fascinated, at the scenery.

After surviving basic training, we boarded another train on our way to Belleville, Ill., for radio mechanic's school. Seven months later, now a radio school graduate, I was boarding a train bound for Tacoma, Wash. This time, I was alone. We were required to travel in uniform, so it wasn't hard to strike up conversations with people who were curious about a girl in uniform, which was relatively rare in the early 1950s. During this two-day trip, as we clattered along, I witnessed scenery I had seen only in pictures.

I miss my former life on trains, but I'm thankful to have such wonderful memories. Years ago, when I started teaching music in Arkansas, we sang a song about trains. Curious, I asked the children how many had ever ridden on a train, and it saddened me to see not one hand go up.

Nancy J. Knight
Fayetteville, Ark.

Rails run away

The city of Cedar Rapids, Iowa, grew and prospered because of the railroads. Now, motorists sit and fume while long freight trains lumber through the heart of downtown. Occasionally, the city council huffs and puffs with indignation. Policemen ticket trainmen for overlong halts on crossings. Then normality returns. The latest attempt to make lemonade out of a lemon has been to plant flower beds along the tracks.

Freight trains were the ride of choice for unemployed men who were looking for work during the Great Depression. They frequently dropped from the train – or were thrown off – and asked townspeople for handouts of food or money.

I like to watch the passing freights and dream of faraway places with strange-sounding names. I am old enough to remember when any conveyance, aside from a horse and buggy, was a breathtaking adventure. Trains were the stuff of fantasy.

The plush seats seemed to me to be the epitome of opulence. They marched, two by two, down each side of the aisle. I was fascinated by the fact a seat could be reversed to provide a cozy nook for four. Even a small child or two could be accommodated.

The Mark Twain Zephyr ran between Burlington, Iowa, and St. Louis. The glass-enclosed dome car was introduced in the 1930s, and it gave one the feeling of being a Rockefeller to ride there at no additional cost. One had a panoramic view of the countryside.

No one that I knew ate in the dining car. It was considered too expensive. If one began a lengthy trip, it was with a well-stocked food basket that was expected to suffice until one's destination was reached. Sandwiches, fried chicken, deviled eggs, cookies and fruit were staples. Beverages depended upon vendors who boarded the train at stops.

Travel has never been an impediment to my ability to sleep. I sleep like the proverbial top. Once, I was reading an exciting mystery when the conductor told me to put out my light.

"It's 8 o'clock," he said, "and time for God-fearing people to be asleep."

Another time, a conductor was assisting passengers to detrain. He grasped my arm with such vigor that my feet never touched the steps. When he let loose, I went flying, to land in an ignominious heap on the brick walkway. With visions of a lawsuit no doubt dancing in their heads, the trainmen rushed to pick me up. I assured them I was fine. A couple of weeks later, a railroad representative phoned to check on me.

In the mid-1930s, 15-year-olds were not sophisticated. When I was to travel from Mobile to Keokuk, Iowa, I had to change trains in St. Louis. My family was afraid I would get lost, and I was firmly instructed to go to the Traveler's Aid office when I got to St. Louis.

I obeyed, and the lady in charge was all atwitter. She said Mrs. Eleanor Roosevelt was in the station and asked if I would like to see her. I had never seen a famous person, so the aid lady and I peeped into Harvey's Restaurant and caught a glimpse of her eating breakfast.

The Roosevelt family came to Burlington when their son Elliott married Miss Ruth Googins. Today, it is claimed that no one in the hinterlands knew that President Roosevelt's legs had been totally incapacitated by infantile paralysis, as polio was called then. Anyone who was at the railroad station that day could see he was standing only because his son James was on one side, and an aide or secret service man was on the other side, holding him upright.

It was exciting when political candidates made whistle stops and appeared on the rear platforms of their campaign trains. I saw President Truman and his daughter, Margaret, when his campaign train stopped in Iowa City, Iowa. Someone presented Margaret with a sheaf of red roses.

Dwight Eisenhower's campaign train stopped in Cedar Rapids. Possibly the crowd's welcome was a trifle warmer for Mrs. Eisenhower than for her husband, as she had lived in Cedar Rapids as a child

Sometimes I wake in the night when a wandering wind blows chill, and I hear a train whistle. It's a freight, but I wish I were on a train – going anywhere.

Ruth Gash Taylor
Cedar Rapids, Iowa

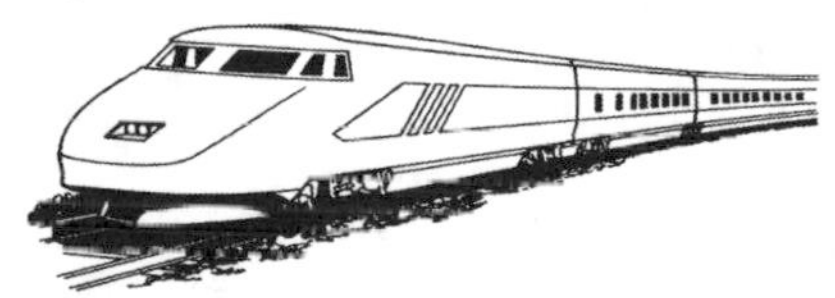

New beginning

I have always liked trains, and I enjoy train trips, long or short. But the one that changed my life, was a trip I took not too long ago from Milford, Conn., to Grand Central Station in New York City.

In order to get to the train tracks at the station, I had

to go up a flight of steps. I was having trouble getting my suitcase up the steps when a nice young man came to my rescue. We talked while we waited for the train. We were traveling on the same train, so we decided to sit together. Throughout the trip we talked and got to know each other. He decided it would be nice if I would meet his grandfather. I agreed to the meeting, and we exchanged names and addresses.

About a month later, I got a phone call from Todd. He asked me if it would be OK for him to bring his grandfather to my home.

We met and had an enjoyable time. A couple of days later, I received a "Thank You" note from Todd's grandfather, Irwin. He said he really enjoyed our visit and wondered if we could get together again. That was the beginning of a new friendship and numerous train trips between New Jersey and Connecticut.

In March 2000, Irwin gave me an engagement ring. We were married in July, with the blessing and cooperation of our families.

Mildred Turner
Clark, N.J.

Hometown history

My father was born in 1881, in Staunton, Ind., and my mother was born in 1897, in Turner, Ind. When they were growing up, they didn't have all the advantages of traveling, entertainment, etc., that we have today. They would go to the train station during the day to see who got on and off the train. To ride the train between these two small towns, about a two-mile ride, cost a dime.

There were passenger coaches and one car they called the miner's car. It made its run at 6 a.m. and 6 p.m. If a miner missed the train, he had to walk to or from work. Trains never stopped for anyone. My grandfathers, father, two uncles and a great-uncle all rode the miner's train to work in the mines.

When Chinook was going to open its mine, about a mile and half southeast of Staunton, the company hired a dozen men for construction work. Beginning April 30, 1928, they were to build a railroad track about a mile east of Staunton, to connect to the main track so the train could get the coal cars from the mine and deliver the coal to the proper locations.

In the 1960s, after the trains had been abandoned, but the railroad tracks still remained, the train crew would leave empty coal cars along the track east of my home. Finally, the mine bought several large trucks to haul the coal from the pit to the tipple for processing and to deliver the coal to the proper locations. My dad was one of the first employees hired to begin the construction work. It was late September 1928, when the first coal was hoisted. Dad retired Jan. 1, 1956.

Dad passed away in October 1956, and my aunt, who lived in Taylorville, Ill., asked my mother and me to spend Thanksgiving Day with her and her family. Since the train didn't stop in Terre Haute, Ind., we were told that if for some reason we changed our plans, we were to call the railroad so the train would not stop. We left Terre Haute on the 4 a.m. train, and went as far as Pana, Ill. My cousin met us at the station and told the station attendant that he would see to it that we were back by 6 p.m. to catch the train back to Terre Haute. He told the attendant that, so he would be sure to let the train crew know to stop in Terre Haute, since they usually didn't.

That trip was my only train ride. If the trains had never been invented, our town of Staunton would never have been the booming town that it once was.

Thelma Wallace
Staunton, Ind.

Good train memories

My mom always told us how she had traveled with her family to Guin, Ala., to see the first train come in on the Frisco Railroad sometime in the early 1880s. She said the headlight looked as if it were as big as the world.

The train was the only way to travel with any speed, so that's the way my parents traveled. They took a train trip from Guin, Ala., to Corenth, Miss., and Mom said that my brother never took his eyes off the beautiful overhead light.

He started talking at an early age, and from the

beginning, Mom said she knew he was trying to ask her something, but she couldn't understand him. He never gave up trying, though. Finally, one day he made her understand that he was asking about the light in the top of the train.

I also got to travel on that train as a child. It was so plush and, oh, those beautiful lights. I traveled on that same train during World War II, across the country during the blackouts.

My grandfather was an engineer in Georgia, and for a long time during the Civil War, he was expected to work without any relief. He kept saying that if someone didn't relieve him soon, he was going to pull into the depot and walk. Nobody listened, so one day he did just that. Another man was put on the train to replace my grandfather, and on that trip, a trestle that had been torn out caused the train to wreck, killing the engineer.

My grandfather went on to become a "sharpshooter" in the Civil War, and he fought in the Battles of Shiloh and Atlanta. He was so impressed with the country around Corenth, Miss., that he went back, bought a few hundred acres of land, and made Corenth his home. That's where my father grew up and studied to be a Pinkerton Man for the railroad. He went to Alabama for a visit, where he met my mom and her family. Mom and Dad fell so in love, that he forgot his love of trains.

I am sad to see our old railroad landmarks go away. At our house, you could hear the whistle, smell the coal smoke, and hear the wheels on the rails when rain was on the way and the wind was from the south.

I used to stand on the platform at the depot with my

parents and watch the trains come and go, along with all the people. Sometimes we would see criminals being loaded on the train to be taken to a prison.

I have good memories of trains.

Edith Shelton
Midway, Texas

The night train

I started teaching in September 1944, in a small town in Iowa. At that time, most 19-year-old girls didn't drive, let alone have cars. Weekends were spent traveling 60 miles on the night train to and from my parents' home.

The train I caught going west left at 1:02 a.m. Then coming back, the train I rode left at 2:20 a.m. Both trips, to and from, required a walk to the train station in the dark.

One winter night, there was a new railroad agent on duty. He offered to sell me a round-trip ticket, but I was not financially prepared to pay cash both ways, so I told him I would buy it, if he would accept my personal check. He told me he could not accept a personal check from a stranger, so I told him I was not a stranger. I pointed out to him where I taught school, where I banked and that I knew almost everyone on Main Street.

Eventually, he agreed to accept my check. I wrote out

the amount and signed my name, Hope C. Robinson. He immediately said that his name also was Robinson. I didn't think much about it, I just figured it might be his way of making conversation.

On Sunday night, when I returned to my teaching town, this same man was standing outside the train, making a mail transfer. When he saw me, he asked how my folks were. He said if I'd wait about five minutes, he'd walk me home. I politely told him "no," and walked off into the darkness.

The next afternoon, after my students were loaded on buses and headed for home, the railroad agent showed up in my schoolroom and invited me to ride the train with him that evening. I later found out that he had just returned to his hometown from England and World War II. He had been discharged and was working as a railroad telegrapher again. His last name really was Robinson.

We later married, and we had seven little Robinsons. We spent 43 years together, and to this day, I still carry the name I was given at birth.

Hope C. Robinson
Perry, Iowa

Riding the rails

In 1937, I left home for Chillicothe, Mo., to attend Chillicothe Business College. I boarded the Chicago &

Northwestern Railway and rode to Omaha, Neb., where I caught the Missouri Pacific Eagle, and continued on to Chillicothe.

I traveled that route many times while in college, and it was an experience I will not forget. In those days, trains zig-zagged all around, picking up and letting off passengers and freight at every little town along the way.

After I graduated from college, I was determined to be a success, so I headed for Chicago to seek my fortune. My dad took me to the train station in Gregory, S.D., and he cried when we parted, saying that this was probably the last time I would be living at home with my family.

Once I arrived in Norfolk, Neb., we had a layover so the conductor could eat lunch. My grandfather met me there and joined me for the remainder of the trip to Chicago. Apparently, my folks had arranged this so there would be someone to watch over their daughter.

Once we got to Chicago, my grandfather saw to it that I got settled in my residence with a friend from college. Then he left for his son's house, where he stayed the whole time I was in Chicago. Eventually, I got homesick, and Grandfather and I took the train home, where my father got me a job at the local bank.

After more than a year in Norfolk, I headed for Washington, D.C., to live with my friend from college again and to serve Uncle Sam. After a couple of years in Washington, I moved to Kansas City, Mo., with my sister.

When we arrived in Missouri, I was met by my special friend from college. We took a few train trips together to his home in Kansas and my home in Nebraska. On one of the trips to my hometown, he asked my father for my hand in marriage. We were married in 1943, and I made many trips on the Eagle to visit my husband, who was in the Air Corps, stationed near St. Louis.

Mostly we drive now, and I am reminded of those many trips on the rails. Sometimes I can't help but mimic the conductor as we drive along through familiar little towns – now ghosts of the past. The rails have been rolled up to make bicycle trails along some routes in Nebraska, but trains were an era of my girlhood that I will forever remember. And the call of the conductor echoes in my mind – "All aboard."

Lorraine Donason Wenger
Gregory, S.D.

Unforgettable

My grandfather worked for the railroad, and once or twice a year, he would get passes for my grandmother and me to travel. We usually went to Buffalo, N.Y., Bradford, Pa., or Johnsonburg, Pa., to visit relatives. Each trip was unique and exciting to me.

I remember waiting in the train station in Mt. Jewett, Pa. There were hard benches on one side of the room and the edges hurt my dangling legs. We carried a large, black, cardboard suitcase with a black handle.

The conductor always stepped down, placed a small stepstool on the ground and helped passengers depart the train. Then he would loudly announce, "Booaard! All Aboard!" We stepped up on the stool, and with the conductor's help, boarded the train. We found a seat and settled in for the trip. The plush covering on the seats made my legs itch. Grandma always sat on the "backward" seat so I wouldn't get sick to my stomach.

The gentle rocking motion and the clickity-clack of the wheels almost made me go to sleep. Then the conductor would come down the aisle, calling out, "Tickets? Tickets, please! Let me have your tickets!" As people gave him their tickets, he punched a little hole in each one with a paper punch, then handed them back.

Before we realized it, the conductor came back down the aisle and loudly announced the next stop. He always reminded everyone to be sure to get all their luggage. The small towns had small, rectangular buildings for stations or depots, but the size of the huge, domed one in Buffalo frightened me. Wherever we went, there was always someone to greet us and give us a big, hearty kiss on the cheek.

Once, I was wearing a bright red coat with heart-shaped pockets on the front and a small, off-to-the-side hat. The conductor called me Little Red Riding Hood, which made me laugh. Just as we were passing the engine, the whistle blew and I started crying. The conductor came over, dried my tears with his large, white handkerchief and comforted me. When I finally smiled, he handed me a nickel and said to have a good time and not to forget him. I never did forget his kindness to a scared little girl, and I never forgot riding on the steam engine trains!

Frances Wolf Williams
Bradford, Pa.

Never forgotten

In the fall of 1917, during World War I, my mother and I took a train trip to visit my aunt and her family on Thanksgiving Day weekend.

Our train was late because the government was using the trains to move troops. This caused us to miss our connection at a small town in southern Kansas. We spent the day waiting for the next train that evening. I was only 8 years old and it was a long, boring day for me.

The outhouse was down the tracks, and I kept my mother busy taking me to and from it. Finally she told me to go by myself. I did, and somebody came by and saw that the door was cracked open, so they shut and locked it. I could not get out.

I yelled for my mother, but she couldn't hear me. I yelled and yelled, but nobody heard me. Finally, a man came by and heard me yelling. He unlocked the door and took me to my mother. I don't think I went to the outhouse any more that day.

To make matters worse, a few weeks later, I broke out with the measles. There was apparently an epidemic of the measles in the army camps. I exposed the entire country school. I ended up giving the measles to more than 40 children.

Lucile Tyree
Topeka, Kan.

My one and only train ride

In the summer of 1941, my mother, father, sisters, grandmother and I boarded a passenger train in Rock Island, Ill., and headed for Oroville, Calif. All his life, my father had been a railroad enthusiast. His growing-up years had been spent on a farm in Missouri, but in his heart, he loved trains. He always wore blue-denim bib overalls, a matching railroad cap, and either a blue or red bandanna stuffed in his left hip pocket. And he always carried his watch in the watch pocket of his bibs.

So, when my uncle wrote and told Dad that he could get a job on the logging train that ran up and down the Feather River Canyon in California, Dad didn't hesitate. He packed us up, sold what he could, gave away what he couldn't, and we were on our way.

I was 5 years old, but to me, it was wonderful to watch the countryside whiz by. Seeing the towns and cities come and go at such a rapid speed was truly amazing. I can remember the three of us girls sleeping in an upper berth, Mom and Dad in the lower berth beneath us and Grandmother in the neighboring lower berth.

We pulled the little curtains closed, and it was like a big camp-out to me and my sisters. We talked and giggled most of the night, because we were too excited to sleep. Our parents had to tell us several times to quiet down, because we were getting too loud and disturbing the neighbors.

Mom and Grandma had packed food for our trip. We had fried chicken, sandwiches, boiled eggs, canned pork and beans, and fruit. We ate, told stories and enjoyed each other's company. It was like a great picnic.

When we got to Denver, Dad got off the train to get a newspaper and stopped to talk to a man standing on the platform. He didn't notice when the train began to leave the station, until Mom shouted out the window. Dad began running and almost missed the train.

On our last day, Dad decided to treat us to dinner in the dining car. Mom took us girls into the bathroom and washed us up, then we put on our Sunday dresses. She reminded us to behave at the table and to mind our manners. When we got there, we marveled at the fancy, white, linen tablecloths, the big, linen napkins we put in our laps, and the waiter, who was dressed in black pants, white jacket and had a towel draped over his arm.

When the waiter sat a small plate filled with little yellow squares in the center of the table, my sister Donna reached over, picked up one of the little squares between her thumb and forefinger, with her pinkie finger arched way up high, and began nibbling daintily away. Dad nudged her under the table and told her that she was about to eat butter, not cheese.

We were back in our regular seats when the train went through the famous Moffett Tunnel. Just as we entered the tunnel, all the lights went out on the train. We thought it was great, but it scared Grandma so bad that she fainted, which scared the rest of us because we knew she had a bad heart. Luckily, there was a doctor on the train, and Grandma came through it just fine.

The rest of the trip was fun, and without further incident. Dad got the job on the logging train as a fireman, but was soon promoted to engineer. Sometimes when he came into the railroad yard to turn his engine around, he would let me and my sisters ride with him on the turntable, before he started back up the mountain. That was the happiest time for all of us.

Helen Wilson
Anderson, Calif.

Miss the sight and sounds

My father was a conductor for the Missouri Pacific. I have many precious memories of him and trains. We had a pass, so going to visit my grandparents in Oklahoma was not a problem. Visiting friends or shopping in the city was fairly easy, too. Many years later, the Stream Liner came through Winfield, Kan. My two older children would ride it to Wichita and spend the day, then ride it back home.

During World War II, many of us went to the depot to see the troops go through – they made a short stop, and the ladies of various organizations distributed cookies to the soldiers.

I remember the call boy who came around calling my father for work. When my father came in from his run, we would race down the street to meet him. If he had been gone overnight, which he usually was, he always had something for us and our mother. I got my start sewing by making clothes for the doll my father brought me from one of his trips.

In 1915 or 1916, my father brought my mother two pairs of bloomers, which had just become fashionable. Hers were one of the first pairs in our little town. The telegrapher at the depot gave much of the day's news to the locals, such as baseball scores and important events. Watching the trains pull in was a social time; people visited among the passengers and each other. With today's technology, it's hard for the younger generation to comprehend all of this.

I have made 17 round trips to California, watching the sunset from the dome car as we sped across the desert. For many years, I changed trains in Barstow and had a layover around midnight. I would take advantage of the restaurant in the Harvey House – one of the last ones on the Sante Fe line.

I had many rewarding experiences. Being a nurse, I

was once asked by the conductor to go to the ladies lounge where a mother and child were. He had already alerted the hospital at Gallup, N.M., to have an ambulance meet the train. I could only offer comfort to them, but it seemed to help. Another time, a mother in the dome car was frantically sewing sequins on a costume her daughter would wear as she competed in a baton-twirling competition in Chicago. She had already won the state competition in California. All of a sudden, the box of sequins slid to the floor. All the passengers quickly dropped to their knees, and in a short time, the mother was back to her sewing. I've often wondered how that youngster did in her competition.

Another time, I was reading in the dome car and half-listening to a conversation between two college students. I heard the girl say something about having the article in her luggage. She said she would be glad to explain it to him in case he would be interested in obtaining one. I was startled when the young man politely asked me if I would keep an eye on his camera equipment. I'm not an expert by any means, but I knew this was costly equipment and said I would watch it for him. The two went off, and I began wondering if they were ever coming back. About four hours later, they returned. I left the dome car for the car I was in, and the couple greeted me with, "Where have you been?" They had paged me, looked through all the cars, including the dome car, where I had been. I'm small, but not invisible!

Trains and their whistles were a part of my life, until about three years ago, when the railroad through our town was discontinued. I'm close to 90 years old, and I'm thankful for the memories of trains and whistles. Even yet, I miss seeing them and hearing their whistle.

Clara Young
Oxford, Kan.

Fond memories

My father worked for the Missouri Pacific Railroad for more than 50 years, so while my sister and I were growing up, we had a pass to ride any of the trains.

When I was 14 and my sister was 12, we boarded the Doodlebug at Eureka, Kan., and went to Emporia, Kan. There, we transferred to another train that took us to Albuquerque, N.M.

Sometimes our family, excluding my father, who worked seven days a week, would get up at 4 a.m. and catch the milk train to Wichita. We'd arrive there at 7 a.m., and walk to Grandmother's house, where breakfast would be waiting for us. After spending the day, we'd catch the 6 p.m. train back home to Neal, Kan.

Years later, when I was in the service, stationed in Cleveland, Ohio, I'd leave on the 8 p.m. train for St. Louis. I'd have a layover there, and then transfer to the Missouri Pacific and arrive in El Dorado, Kan., the next morning, where my father would meet me.

Betty Whiteside
Potwin, Kan.

152
MKT
MKT

Chapter 5
History

The Silver Streak

The train was called the Silver Streak. Its first locomotives were called the Silver King, Silver Queen, Silver Knight and Silver Princess. Later locomotives were called the Silver Bullet, Silver Comet, Silver Clipper and a veritable host of other "Silvers." It was, of course, the Burlington Zephyr.

During the mid-1930s, one of the highlights of my young life was to ride my new bike down to the embankment that overlooked the Chicago, Burlington and Quincy Railroad Co. tracks to watch those silver trains streak by. I wasn't alone. Sometimes it seemed as if the whole town of Rochelle, Ill., was there. We sat in the sun on green grass in the summer, or stood in the grayness of winter snow, waiting for the distant rumble. We leaned forward breathlessly to be the first to catch sight of the magnificent, eerily quiet, streamlined marvel.

The railroad was founded in 1849 as the Aurora Branch Railroad. Gradually it ranged farther and farther afield from Aurora, Ill., reaching Quincy, Ill., and then Burlington, Iowa. Its headquarters remained in

Aurora into the last quarter of this century as it covered much of the midwest, competing with the Chicago and Northwestern Railroad.

The first diesel-powered stainless steel locomotive in America was built for the CB&Q by the E.G. Budd Manufacturing Co. of Philadelphia. It made its first run April 9, 1934, to Perkiomen Junction and returned to Philadelphia. On April 18th, at the Broad Street Station in Philadelphia, it was christened the "Burlington Zephyr."

The origin of the name is interesting. It was taken from Geoffrey Chaucer's Prologue to "The Canterbury Tales" written in the 14th century. A modern English translation by J.J. Nicolson in 1934, goes like this:

When April with his showers sweet with fruit
The drought of March has pierced unto the root
And bathed each vein with liquor that has power
To generate therein and sire the flower;
When Zephyr also has, with his sweet breath,
Quickened again, in every holt and heath,
The tender shoots and buds, and ...

The Silver Streak made history May 26, 1934, when it ran nonstop from Denver to Chicago, a distance of 1,015.4 miles, in 13 hours, 5 minutes and 44 seconds. This cut the normal time almost exactly in half and bested the previous record of 58 mph for a 401-mile run set by the Royal Scot on the London to Edinburgh run in 1928.

Fourteen trainmen crewed the train. There were three engineers, four pilots, four road foremen, a conductor, a dining car inspector and a radioman. They reached a top speed of 112.5 mph during a three-mile stretch from Yuma to Schramm, Colo. The average speed for the run was 79.1 mph. A total of 418 gallons of diesel fuel was consumed, at four cents per gallon, for a total cost of $16.72.

The track for the entire thousand miles was guarded by local law enforcement officers, the American Legion and the Boy Scouts. All other trains were side-tracked. The switches were all spiked to prevent tampering. Flagmen cleared every road crossing from Denver to Chicago.

After its arrival at the Halsted Street Station in Chicago, it wound its way over city tracks to Chicago's lake front and the Century of Progress World's Fair, then in its second year.

During the long reign of the Silver Streak, up to 1968, about 225 Zephyrs were manufactured and put into service. But the ones I remember, are those I saw during the Depression years when I waited eagerly for them to purr through my town.

Birney Dibble
Eau Claire, Wis.

The 1949 train wreck

As a child, people always asked me if the sound of the train whistles near our house ever woke me up. But I never even noticed them – they were so familiar to us.

My family and I lived in a house only a few yards from the railroad tracks where the Westbound Southern Railway passenger train, No. 15, wrecked. I was only 4 years old at the time, but as I got older, my father told me all about that fateful day.

It was a foggy Monday morning, Sept. 19, 1949. The westbound first-class passenger train, the No. 15, was carrying approximately 40 passengers and several crew members. The train consisted of diesel-electric units 4134A and 4352B, a mail car, a passenger-baggage car, a coach car, a dining car, two express cars and four sleeping cars.

J.E. "Jake" Smyre, a railway mail worker, reported in his statement that the crew members began to suspect trouble when they realized that they had made the run from Catawba to Claremont, S.C., in four minutes. The same route that normally took them a little over five minutes. Reports also show that Jake stated that the train left Salisbury at 3:10 a.m., and around 5:20 a.m., the train was within three blocks of the depot in Newton, S.C., but when they came to Rowe's Crossing, they failed to make the horseshoe curve and jumped the tracks.

When the two engines jumped the tracks, they took with them the Railway Post Office car, two storage mail cars, a Railway Express car, a baggage-passenger car and the dining car. Six pullman and coach cars remained on the track, upright, and rolled to a stop near the depot. People appeared from everywhere to offer assistance doing whatever they could.

My father, who worked for the Southern Railway,

along with my mother, shielded me from seeing the bodies of the injured and the dead. There were three members of the crew who were killed, two cooks and the fireman, who died at the hospital the next day. In addition, 34 passengers were injured. At some point, we heard that two of the surviving crew members had to have their legs amputated from injuries sustained in the wreck.

A 2-month-old baby, who had been thrown from the car, was found unharmed, sleeping soundly, lying in a field some distance from the train. Her mother and 2-year-old sister were taken to the hospital and admitted for treatment.

Reports showed that the cause of the wreck was due to excessive speed on a curve. The throttle was said to have been frozen at 94 miles per hour. When asked about the speed, the engineer stated that he took precautions to slow the train down when the fireman warned him that they were moving too fast. But he was blamed anyway, and was dismissed from duty.

The wreck did not affect my desire to ride trains, however. I figure there could be an accident no matter how you travel. My interest in railroading grew over the years. I was saddened over the loss of passenger trains in my area.

Alma Isaac Kiziah
Granite Falls, N.C.

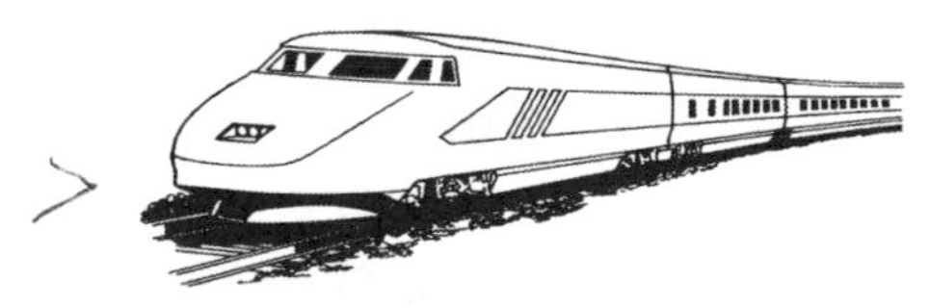

The story of the wreck of the Old 97

Driving along on U.S. 58, through Danville, Va., I'm reminded by a marker, that this was the spot where the most famous train wreck in American history occurred.

It was on a hot, steamy afternoon in late September 1903, when Old 97, a five-car mail express train, left Monroe, Va., to go south. Monroe is a small community in the Piedmont section of Virginia and a few miles north of Lynchburg.

Steve Broady, the engineer of Old 97, was taking the train to Spencer, N.C. This town is located between Greensboro and Charlotte, just off I-85. However, the departure from Monroe was late. Knowing this, Mr. Broady gave the engine "full throttle."

In the early 1900s, all locomotives were driven by steam. They had an attached tender that carried the coal and water needed to make the steam. This was a job tended to by the fireman. The engineer, perched high in the cab, operated the huge contraption with various levers and controls.

Knowing that the train was behind schedule, Broady tried to make up the lost time between Lynchburg and Danville. He called to his fireman to throw more coal in the firebox. This produced more steam and more power.

Going downhill from White Oak Mountain, some 12 miles north of Danville, the train reached a speed of 90 miles an hour. This was entirely too fast, but the engineer was planning to slow down as he approached the outskirts of Danville, a small, sleepy cotton mill town located on the Dan River in southside Virginia.

The air brakes on Old 97 failed. Realizing the train could not make the curve next to the Dan River Mills Inc. building on the river, the brave engineer did the next best thing that he knew to do. He pulled hard on the whistle to warn anyone in harm's way. The doomed train careened from the high wooden trestle, left the tracks and wrecked next to the mill. Mr. Broady, along with eight others, died in the wreck.

"The Wreck of the Old 97" became a hit song soon thereafter. It is still popular today among bluegrass music fans.

William O. Murray
Danville, Va.

Dalton gang experience

My grandmother and grandfather made the Oklahoma Land Run in April 1889 with their three small boys. In the spring of 1890, Grandmother returned to her father's farm in Kansas, with her three boys, to collect some household items.

On their return to Guthrie, Okla., they boarded the Santa Fe train. On June 1, 1890, while traveling through Red Rock, Okla., the train was stopped and held up by the Dalton gang. The outlaws went through the passenger car and collected money and other valuables from all of the passengers. When they got to my grandmother and her sons, one of the gang members said, "Ma'am, we don't want anything from you."

About three months later, my grandmother's 5-year-old son came running into the house and said, "Ma, those men who robbed the train just watered their horses here." She went to the door and saw the Dalton gang headed toward the Cimarron River.

Jane C. Waldroop
Norman, Okla.

The call

The wild eerie whistle of a freight train
Lumbering toward the distant west
Pierces through the lonely night
Stirring quiet hearts with vague unrest.

Wanderlust souls heed the call to adventure
Down winding road or silver track
Sometimes they stop by a glowing hearth
Until a poignant whistle lures them back.

Lynda Schlomann
St. James, Minn.

Chapter 6
Traveling Tots

Train trip mishap

After spending two weeks in northern Minnesota with my two cousins on their farm, the three of us boarded a train to go back to my home in Minneapolis. It was the summer of 1941, and I was 8 years old. For some reason, I decided to close the train window. When I did, it slammed down on the little finger of my left hand, and the two side latches both latched.

We must have created quite a commotion, because in no time, some of the train employees were standing there prying the window open. I can still see the pry bar splintering away the wood from the window sill as it released my little finger.

The first thing my parents saw when we got off the train at the Great Northern Depot, in Minneapolis, were my two cousins carrying all of our luggage. I was behind them carrying my left hand in my right hand, with my little finger bandaged and sticking straight up in front of me like a candle.

My next train ride occurred in 1945, when I was 12 years old. My buddy and I rode the street car downtown to the same massive granite depot, where we were to board the Great Northern and ride across the river.

The conductor asked us where we were going, and we told him we were only going as far as St. Paul. We explained our love of trains, and he offered to let us ride in the observation car. We gratefully accepted, and were taken to the last car of the train, which seemed to us more like a living room. The rich businessmen riding there were friendly to us, and that kindness impressed me deeply.

Both train rides were most certainly memorable, and the awesome granite depot in St. Paul still stands today.

Duane Anderson
Eagan, Minn.

Dad to the rescue

I grew up in a big family with no car in the 1920s. Dad worked for the railroad, so when we went anywhere, we went by train. We would travel about 17 miles to Lincoln, Neb. The train would leave our town at 4 p.m. and return at midnight.

One time, my dad took my sister and me with him to Minden, Neb., because he knew how much we loved to ride the train. During the trip, my sister and I went to the restroom, and while we were in there, the train stopped at a depot and the door locked.

We were just starting to panic when the door unlocked, and there stood Dad. I guess he thought we should have been back sooner, so lucky for us, he asked the conductor to unlock the door so we could get out. When we got to our destination, we had a nice visit with our aunt and then headed for home.

Anna Birt
Hickman, Neb.

Noisy train ride

When my fiance got home from Alaska for a furlough, in April 1945, we decided to get married. When he reported back to duty, he was sent to New York City. He wanted us to be together, so I boarded a passenger train in Steubenville, Ohio, and set forth to be with my new husband.

I was only 17 1/2 years old, and this was my very first train trip. I was really glad to find that our neighbor's daughter was also on board, along with her 1-year-old son. The boy cried most of the trip, and she was afraid they were going to put her off the train. As I was the oldest of six children, I tried to help soothe him, but to no avail.

A few days after I had arrived at Grand Central Station for a happy reunion with my husband, I received a letter from my train companion. The letter said, "Hope you've had the measles!" That's why her son had been crying, he had the measles. And luckily, so had I.

My husband and I have been married for 55 years now. Now that he's retired, after his knee is healed from a knee replacement, hopefully we'll get to do some traveling.

Grace Fox
Morganton, N.C.

An adventure for children

We were to take a trip to California on the train!

To cross the Unites States by train in the 1930s was as thrilling to children then as a voyage into outer space might be today. From our home in Detroit, we eagerly looked forward to this exciting adventure.

My older brother and I had just recovered from bouts of whooping cough, and our parents believed a visit to the sunny West Coast would work its magic on us. In addition, we would meet several relatives. Of course, we also had heard a lot about Hollywood and certainly hoped we would see some stars.

It was fun packing our suitcases and going down to the old Michigan Central Station in Detroit for our train trip to Chicago. Our papa had to stay home to work, but he was there to wave goodbye as we left with our mother and grandmother on the first leg of our journey.

Arriving in Chicago, we were shuttled clear across town from one huge railroad station to another even larger station, where cross-country train trips began.

We enjoyed sitting on benches in the huge waiting room, hearing trains being announced and watching passengers lining up and hurrying off to their trains.

Then the loud, squawky public address system announced our train, and it was time for us to board the Santa Fe Super Chief for our 40-hour, 2,000 plus-mile trip.

We hurried down the concourse to the track where our sleek train was waiting, while the sturdy red cap brought along our luggage. The conductor, with his cap and brass buttons and big watch, placed a metal step stool on the platform and helped us climb up into the train. It appeared very large and imposing to us children. We found our seats in the Pullman car and eagerly awaited departure. The conductor checked our tickets, and we were on our way at last. We felt very comfortable. Ventilation in our car was good as were temperature and humidity. There was plenty of room, and large, soft pillows were provided. The ride was clean, quiet and smooth. We spent a lot of our time looking out the windows, of course, and we also read and played games. When we became tired, we would nap.

Fellow passengers fascinated us. After spending so much time together, we got acquainted. There was a very stunning-looking girl on her way to Hollywood to get in the films. Card games were very popular. We only watched. One gambler turned out to be a card shark. We heard that one night after winning from several people, he got off at a stop in the middle of the night and never came back.

To this day, many highlights and experiences stand

out in our minds. Passing over bridges and trestles, along grades and through tunnels was exciting. When the train went around a big curve, we could look out the window and see our own engine up ahead.

A great way to see more of the country was to return via another route. The conductor would tell us when some unusual sight was coming up so we could watch for it. On the Northern Route, we went across the Great Salt Lake Cutoff, which became monotonous as it involved the largest bridge, 12 miles long. The great desert and sights like El Canyon Diablo were fascinating to look for in the Southwest.

Conductors and porters changed at division points. They all were very courteous and pleasant, as were all the dining car waiters. The conductor called out station stops where passengers could get off briefly. When we pulled into a station for a brief stop, the candy butcher would come aboard the train with a large tray slung from a cord around his shoulders and sell candy, nuts, newspapers, magazines and small souvenirs. Some of the Native American silver jewelry was lovely, often set with turquoise stones and Mexican "fire opals."

If we wanted to stretch our legs on the train, we would go get a drink of water from the fountain at the end of each car. You pulled a little paper triangle from the dispenser and pinched it open into a small cup. It was tricky trying to drink while the train car swayed and jiggled.

Passenger rail service in the United States between the two world wars was never more luxurious, and meals in the diner were excellent. We would walk through the cars to the diner and were always thrilled as the connecting metal floor plates would shift and rattle while we tried to pull open the heavy doors.

The diner was just like being in a fine restaurant with elegant appointments, china and silver, and fine linens complementing delicious food ordered from a large menu. For example, a glass of tomato juice was served surrounded by a huge bowl of cracked ice. We were certain the famed Orient Express had nothing better. Of course, this was quite costly, as a full breakfast was 25 cents, lunch was at least 30 cents and a three-course dinner could cost as much as 50 cents. They had special "teas" for children on their own menu.

When it was time for bed, we never grew tired of watching the porter make up the berths. We could call the porter with a handy bell by our window. He took a huge key to open up and let down the upper berth, which was used in the daytime for storing the bedding. The ingenious design quickly transformed daytime seats into double-decker, comfortable beds with crisp white sheets and warm blankets. Our bags went on a shelf and we put our clothes into a little woven hammock. A safety ladder was provided for the top passenger. There was only one problem – if you forgot and suddenly sat up, you would bang your head. For extra cost, one could ride in a private drawing room or compartment.

It sometimes was hard to go to sleep right away. Once we were buttoned in behind the thick curtains, it was such fun to run up the window shade over our berth and look out at the night. We would see gates and flashing lights at intersections as cars waited for our train to rush by.

One night, we woke up when the train was backing up very rapidly. An inquiry revealed that we were on the wrong track and were trying to get on a siding, out of the way of the Limited before it rushed through.

One evening, our train paused for just a few minutes at Albuquerque, N.M., and there was our Aunt Clara and Uncle Bert waiting for us on the platform.

Our return trip was equally thrilling. When we arrived home at last, Papa was waiting on the platform to greet us. He said we had grown and were the picture of health and full of sunshine. Now we considered ourselves seasoned travelers, and we were eager to share all our interesting experiences with our friends, neighbors, relatives and schoolmates.

Many years and many train trips have not erased our fond memories of this first luxurious train ride.

George and Mary Green
(Brother and sister)
Dearborn, Mich., and Toledo, Ohio

Another chance

About 30 years ago, my husband and I, along with his mother and our 4-month-old son, took a three-day train trip. This was a very memorable trip.

Our son was fussy, so we tried everything to keep him

happy. We did not use disposable diapers. We had to heat his bottles and baby food jars using the hot water in a small sink. He slept in a hammock affair with a hard board in the bottom suspended over my small bed. One night, the whole thing fell on top of me.

In spite of that trip, my husband and I still like trains and are looking forward to taking another trip, now that he is retired. This time it will be just the two of us.

Jeannie Heverling
Bellingham, Wash.

Family trip

In 1961, the company my husband worked for transferred us to Fremont, Calif. I left with tears in my eyes, as I was leaving my parents and sisters. California seemed so far away from Missouri, where my husband and I were raised, married and started our family.

We'd been in California for a couple of years, when my mother broke her hip. Naturally, I wanted to go home to see her. We had three children and not much money, so flying was out. We didn't know if our car would make the trip, so we decided to go by train.

The trip would take two days and two nights. We started out, loaded down with books, crayons, games, snacks and three very excited children, ages 7, 10 and 11. The scenery around Lake Tahoe and through the mountains in the western states was beautiful.

The children managed to stay occupied with the activities and snacks we brought. They enjoyed walking back and forth through the cars to the caboose. There was a dome car on the train, but it wasn't air conditioned, so you couldn't stand the heat very long.

The most exciting thing to the children was going to the dining car for meals. We didn't go out to eat as a family very often, and when we did, it was to a fast-food place. To go into a dining car, with white tablecloths, and to be waited on, was a real treat.

When it came to sleeping, the children had no trouble at all. They slept so sound, they didn't even hear the train stopping and starting during the night. However, it wasn't so easy for mom and dad. After two nights of sleeping in our seats, we were ready for a bed.

All in all, we had a great trip. When we arrived in California, we felt we were seasoned train travelers. To this day, our now-grown children still talk about their first train ride.

Jean Hieken
Merrimack, N.H.

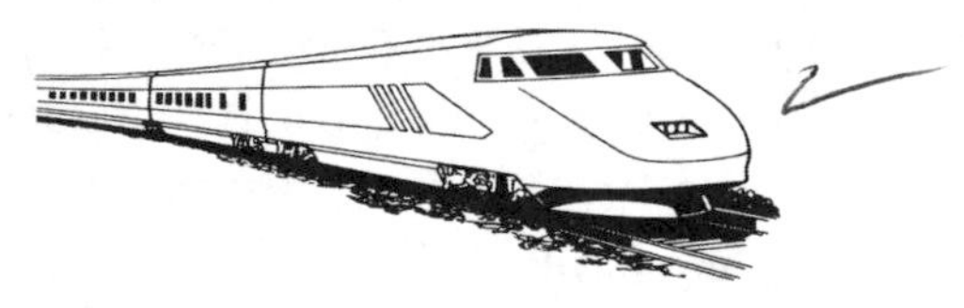

Impatient

When I was a small girl, my mother, older sister and I would ride the train to visit my grandmother. Mother wouldn't tell me we were going until a couple of days ahead of time, because I would be ready to start packing the suitcase.

Mother would pack our lunch in a shoe box, and Dad would drive us the nine miles to town, where we caught the train. As soon as we got on the train and found our seats, I was ready to eat. We stuck our heads out the window of the train, so we couldn't wear good clothes because the coal dust got all over us.

A while back, I had the opportunity to ride Amtrak from Seattle to Fort Worth, Texas, and it brought back a lot of childhood memories. I enjoyed that last train trip so much, that I'm already planning to take another one.

Virginia Bennett
Mead, Okla.

Still fascinated by trains

My first memory is living in a cabin on a hill overlooking the railroad tracks, miles off the beaten path in Southwest Georgia. I was about 4 years old at the time, a shy, freckled-face kid with my head in the clouds. Our nearest neighbors were sharecroppers on the other side of a cornfield with a little girl my age. We were the best of friends and stuck together like glue.

Many afternoons she and I sat on my rickety steps and listened to the rumble of a Southern Pacific freight train speeding down the tracks. In seconds, it changed from a far-off vibration to a clickity-clack, thunder-like noise 500 feet from us. In passing, the train whistle would toot as the conductor waved to us in an instamatic blur of speed and L&N boxcars. With our hands clasped tightly over our ears, we wouldn't move a muscle until the red caboose disappeared out of sight.

Thinking back, that's when I felt the first stirrings of restlessness taking hold. Even then, I wanted to climb aboard that smoke-belching locomotive and ride the rails to exciting distant places. But my friend wasn't a dreamer like me, she wanted to play. We would sit on the ground and share a cup of "tea," which was actually water from a nearby spring. In my own little world, I'd pretend I was all dressed up in a satin gown on a train bound for unknown adventures.

Dreaming aside, sometimes old hobos, unshaven and dirty, would hop down from the train and wander up the grassy slope to our back door in search of a tiny morsel of food. My mother would oblige with a cup of hot soup and a chunk of cornbread, looking past the ragged clothes to a hungry soul down on his luck. Her Christian belief was that no one should go hungry in this land of plenty.

In 1956, after my sixth birthday and before I started first grade, my cousin, Annie, came to visit. She rode a passenger train all the way from Riverside Junction, not more than 20 miles away, although to me it seemed like a hundred. Man, was I impressed! Annie was old, in her 20s. When she was ready to return home, I, being the youngest of three siblings and considered the "baby," threw a tantrum because I wanted to go with her, and I finally got my chance to ride the train.

We crossed a trestle high above the Chattahoochee, snaking its way southward between the Alabama and Georgia state lines. I pressed my nose against the window and gazed down at moss-covered oaks and clumps of sycamore trees hugging the banks of that muddy river. I remember a lonesome whistle and the pungent smell of the coal-burning engine.

But if I were asked today what I did on my first trip away from home, I couldn't say. I do recall arriving back home safe and sound, bubbling over with stories to tell my friend. To this day, her name escapes me, yet I'm still fascinated with trains.

On a recent trip to Missouri, my husband and I stood in line at the Branson Scenic Railway, with a crowd of enthusiastic tourists. I stared at the silver Kansas City Southern, and heard the conductor shout, "All aboard!" We climbed on and settled down in the dining car as the train rumbled its way over a trestle high above the Ozark mountains. I looked down at the rocky valleys below and realized I was a long way from the south land and my first train ride across the Chattahoochee. And just like that old river back home, I'm still a restless spirit winding my way through the twists and turns of life.

Flo Kellogg
Silver Springs, Fla.

A nickel each way

When I was a child, in the mid-1920s, we lived in an oil camp in Canova, Ark. This was before the days of school buses, so my brother and I had to ride the train back and forth to school everyday. My parents entrusted my brother with the train fare, which was five cents apiece each way, because he was a couple of years older than me.

One day, after school, when I was 10, my brother was late getting to the train, because he was playing ball. I could hear the train coming and began to cry, thinking I would never get home to see my mother again. Well, lucky for me, a lady from the Salvation Army met the train daily to greet the departing passengers. She saw me crying and asked me what was wrong. I told her my sad story, and she gave me a nickel out of her tambourine, so I could get home.

When I got off the train, Mom saw I was crying and didn't see my brother. She thought something terrible had happened. Of course, I told her, with flowing tears, that it was the worst thing that had ever happened to me. My brother ended up walking the five miles home and got a good tongue lashing from my dad, who informed him that it had better never happen again.

This did not pacify me, however, so I kept the tears coming, and to make me feel better, my dad said I could start carrying my own train fare. Well, the next morning, I had fifteen cents in my pocket – ten cents for train fare and five cents to put back in the Salvation Army tambourine.

Now, when my brother and I get together, we talk about our childhood and have many good laughs. This story is just one of the many wonderful memories I have of the "good ole days."

Esta Wills
Wichita, Kan.

Envied by friends

When I was a small child, approximately 70 years ago, my father was a conductor on the Norfolk and Western Railroad. We lived close to the railroad tracks, with an overhead bridge, and all of the neighborhood children would come running when we heard the train whistle. We would wave to the passengers, and we were thrilled when they waved back.

Our friends envied my siblings and me because we could ride the train free. Daddy had to secure trip passes for us. However, he and Mom had annual passes.

Vacation time meant a train ride to our destination. My sister and I always enjoyed going to the bathroom on the train and seeing the sign that read: "Do not flush the hopper while the train is in the station." We would giggle over the word "hopper" – that was a new word in our vocabulary.

About 10 years after I got married, I was visiting my parents with my two small boys. My father, although retired from the railroad, thought the boys should ride the train. All of the other grandchildren had already experienced the opportunity. He made arrangements for a short train trip, and our sons were thrilled at the new experience.

They got their next opportunity to ride the train a few years later, when they were 8 and 10. It was 1959, and my husband and I, along with our sons, were leaving for the Philippine Islands, taking a ship out of San Francisco.

We purposely chose to travel by train from Winston-Salem, N.C., to San Francisco. The boys were very excited. They had remembered the short trip with their grandpa. They figured this trip, which would last from Friday afternoon until Monday morning, would really be neat. They wondered what could be better than sleeping in our own compartment and eating our meals in the dining car.

Since our trip was scheduled for Easter weekend, I purchased two Easter baskets to give the boys on Sunday morning. What a nice surprise it was for them to wake up with a beautiful basket of goodies beside their bunk beds. "Here comes Peter Cottontail hopping down the railroad trail."

Once we arrived in the dining car for Easter breakfast, we were greeted by our smiling waiter, who told us, "Happy Easter." We had a delicious meal, then returned to our compartment and discussed the real meaning of the holiday. As we were singing softly, there was a knock on our door. It was our waiter holding four brightly dyed eggs for the boys.

It was a good day for the boys. We hid eggs a big part

of the day. The boys stayed in the bathroom while I hid the eggs, then we took turns hiding them. We all had a good time, and this train trip still has memories for our family.

Mrs. James (Mary) Lochridge Sr.
Albany, Ga.

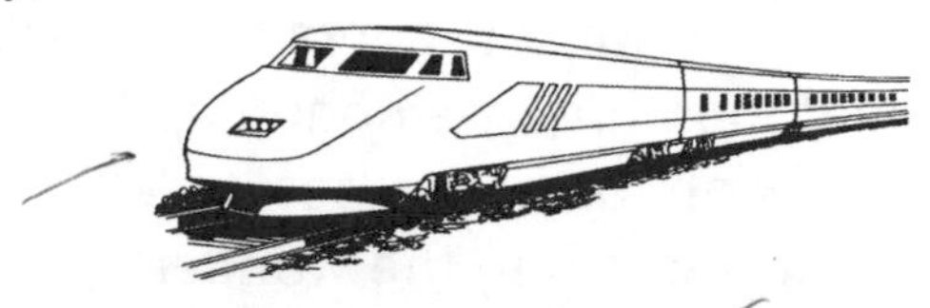

A ride in the caboose

In 1913, my mom, 3-year-old sister, infant brother and I boarded a train for Nebraska. We rode about 20 miles, then had to change trains to go to Lincoln, Neb. It was after dark when we boarded our next train, and a few miles down the tracks, the conductor came through the cars checking tickets.

He looked at Mom's ticket, and told her we were on the wrong train. He said we'd have to go back to the last station and catch the right train from there. Of course, the next train for Lincoln, Neb., wasn't leaving until the following day. Mom told the conductor that we had no money for a hotel.

The conductor disappeared, then returned a few minutes later. He said they had wired the train we were supposed to be on, and it would stop and wait for us. Within a few minutes, our train was stopped next to the train we should have caught. We boarded and were relieved to be going in the right direction.

Our train arrived in Lincoln, Neb., behind schedule,

and we missed our next train. We spent the night in the train depot, and the next morning, a brakeman approached Mom and said that if we wouldn't mind riding in the caboose of a freight train, that it was leaving immediately.

What an experience! The caboose had a wooden seat along one side, where we sat. There was a small stove in the center, and soon after we boarded, the conductor put a piece of steak on top of the hot stove. I remember hearing it sizzle and smelling the wonderful aroma.

When the steak was done cooking, the conductor cut a piece off for himself, then put the rest on a platter, which he handed to my mom.

He took a loaf of bread from the cupboard and tore it in half, again sharing with Mom. Oh, how we enjoyed that breakfast, and the rest of our trip.

Many years later, my husband and I were driving through Nebraska and saw a museum with a caboose. We stopped and toured the old, weathered railroad car, and it looked just like the one I had ridden in when I was only 6 years old.

Irene Wyant
Stevenson, Wash.

My special trains

When I was a child in a small town,
I'd lay at night and listen to the sound
Of the clickety-clack, clickety-clack,
Of train wheels on the railroad track.

As it pulled to a stop, I'd hear escaping steam.
Hear it pulse as if alive, and it would seem
It couldn't wait to be gone again,
And showed impatience with mere men.

There was a sound of a whistle as it pulled away,
I could almost see the cars as they swayed.
And again, I hear the clickety-clack
Of train wheels on the railroad track.

In the distance I could hear the whistle
As it traveled through land of cactus and thistle.
As it beckoned to travelers, I could hear the moan
Of that heavy engine, born to ever roam.

I love the sound of a train rushing by,
Seems the stars give echo as they shine on high.
But I was earthbound and must stay at home,
Too young but to listen to the engine's moan.

Ruby O. Davis
Denver, Colo.

ST. PAUL, KANSAS

CO.
377
377

Chapter 7
Hobos

Daddy's friendship with the hobos

During the Depression days, and for 30 years, my father was a telegraph operator for the Chicago and North Western Railway, in an office called, "Tower Z," in Missouri Valley, Iowa. He was a kind-hearted man, and many men, called hobos, rode the rails in boxcars looking for work.

The hobos would stop in at the tower to get warm by the fire, in winter, or to ask where they could get something to eat. A lot of times, if he thought they were good men, Daddy would send them the three blocks to our house, where Mom would feed them. They were all well-mannered, and appreciative of the kindness and hospitality.

One afternoon, my father sent a man to our house for something to eat, and I was so happy! He looked just like Santa Claus. He had a long, white beard, and he was plump.

When I saw him, I said, "Santa! What are you doing down here at our house, you're supposed to be at the North Pole!"

He laughed and told me he just thought he'd drop in

to see me and my brother.

Mom gave him a good lunch and he left.

Meanwhile, the night watchman and two policemen went to see my father, asking if he had seen an old man with a long, white beard come through. Dad said he had, and that he had sent him to our house for a good meal, before the man caught the next freight train, going west. That was the last time my father ever sent any hoboes to our house for a good meal. "Santa Claus" was wanted by the police; he had escaped from prison in Kentucky.

Helen Barker
Eureka Springs, Ark.

Unforgettable hobos

I was born and raised in a small town in Michigan, in the Upper Peninsula. It was Iron Ore country where my father worked in the mines for 50 years. Our house, which was about 40 feet from the railroad tracks, would shake as the trains rolled by. Trains carrying iron ores passed every hour, every day, with both full and empty loads.

The sound of the trains was a lullaby to us as babies. Then as we grew older, my siblings and I would chant "I think it can, I thought it could, I knew it would," as the train pulled nearly a hundred cars behind it, on an upgrade. We would stand on our front porch and wave to the engineers and wait eagerly for them to wave back. Although we never actually talked to the engineers or got to meet them, we felt like they were family.

I remember the hobos who hopped the trains. They would jump off near our house and beg for food. My mother always fixed something for them, and they would sit on our porch and talk to us while they ate. They were always thankful and polite, and we were never afraid of them. In later years, they weren't allowed to hop the trains because there were too many of them, and some would cause trouble.

During my childhood days, I rode a couple of trains, and it was a thrill. How well I recall the pleasure I derived from trains, as they have always been close to me. While growing up, we always lived near the tracks, and when I got married and moved to South Dakota, we had tracks across our land. Even now, I only live three blocks from the tracks, and when I walk to town, I still like to count the cars and wave to the engineer. God bless them.

Doris Murtha
Woonsocket, S.D.

Freight-hopping memories

I began hopping freights when I was 10 years old. Of course, I had ridden the freights for fun as a 9-year-old, but only for short trips. By the time I was 15 years old,

I had hopped more freight trains with unknown destinations, that I marvel at how agile I was then. I am amazed today that I wasn't killed or maimed.

In those perilous days, I wasn't afraid of anything or anybody. I remember my first lesson in freight hopping. A freight train was pulling out of the Missouri Pacific yards at about 25 miles per hour, a little fast. I grabbed for the ladder to climb to the top of a boxcar, but slipped and fell, my right arm landing on the track. The wheels clickety-clacked, swiftly now. I jerked my arm off the track and rolled off the gravel tie bed.

I get the shivers now when I think how close I came to getting my arm cut off by a boxcar wheel. Why would an American boy in his early teens run that kind of risk? The answer was easy. We were the urchins of the great Depression.

When I kissed my mother goodbye one summer morning in 1935, I caught an outbound freight. The eight-wheel steam engine blew a cloud of smoke and cinders in heavy strain to pull 50 or 60 boxcars.

I ran full tilt, and finally someone grabbed my wrists to pull me into the boxcar. It was a young hobo around my age.

"Jeez, Bo," he said, "I thought you were a goner."

I thanked him as my eyes cleared to see 11 other youths in the dark corners of that boxcar. Juvenile hobos were human discards who came from farms and inner cities. We all had the same goals – to relieve our families of the burdens to care for us and to find a job. That year, unknown to me, of course, a Chicago research group estimated the juvenile hobo population at a half-million between the ages of 11 and 17. Some had not attended high school.

"God is guts – He keeps you pushing on," a young hobo, who went by the name Blink, once said. And it's something I will never forget. Blink had a patch over his left eye, which had been burned out by a hot cinder.

Dewey Linze
Gardnerville, Nev.

Hobo code

When I was a little girl, we lived on a farm where the railroad ran behind our grove and apple orchard. As a result of living so close to town, and to the railroad, we had a lot of hobos come to our door.

My mother always gave them something to eat. I asked her one day why there were always so many hobos around our house. She told me they put some sort of marks on the trees, telling other hobos that they could get a meal at the house. We also had a lot of gypsies come to our farm wanting to bargain for chickens or whatever they could get.

There was a beet dump on the train line, just across the road from the county school I went to. One of the students' mother worked in the office, so at recess and lunch, we would run over there. If we were late getting back, however, there were consequences, not to our liking. I guess we never learned because we kept right on sneaking over there.

One day during World War I, my mother told us to go outside and watch for the train to go by. She said her brother was supposed to be on it, headed for his Army camp. I was fascinated by trains, and still am.

Lenora Kiewiet
Buffalo Center, Iowa

Memories of Sweetwater's Hobo Springs from 1941-1949

I'm sitting here at Hobo Springs, down by the railroad tracks, with memories and pictures in my mind of long ago. I can still see the old freight trains coming down the tracks, the hobos riding along under the old black smoke.

All through the night you could hear the rumble of the trains and their whistles blowing as they went by Hobo Springs and the sheep farm of F.A. McCosh, three miles south of Sweetwater, Tenn. The old Hobo Springs is where the hobos would get off the train to get a drink of spring water while the trains filled the old boiler up at the water tank.

There were freight trains, passenger trains, mail trains and troop trains carrying soldiers during World War II. They all ran by the old Hobo Springs, the sheep farm and the old farmhouse that stood nearby.

The hobos sometimes played cards and rolled dice while they waited for the train to fill up with water or switch tracks for another train to go by. Or sometimes it was because they had to wait until the brakeman was out of sight, so they could climb back on and ride. Sometimes they ended up staying overnight, sleeping in the old farm barn.

The hobos would sometimes go by the back door of the farmhouse and ask for food or a place to sleep.

Hobo Springs and the sheep farm will always be a memory for me. I was only 6 years old, but I still remember those days, because I was the lad who lived in that old farmhouse on the sheep farm. Hobo Springs is a legend now, just like Jimmy Rodgers, when he sang about the blues and hobos, and the trains he hoboed and rode.

Today, those songs and stories live on. Hobo Springs is still there, by the railroad tracks and the farm, but the hobos and sheep are gone. Only in the memories of yesteryear, from 1941-1949, do they live on.

Ralph W. Robinson
Sweetwater, Tenn.

Progress

In the late 1930s and early 1940s, my parents lived just a few hundred yards from the MN&A Railroad. My grandfather and great uncle helped lay the tracks.

When I was 5 or 6 years old, I remember my mother feeding the hobos who came up the hill to our house. There was a trestle below our house where they camped. I remember some were dirty and scary-looking, but Mom never turned one away without a meal. We were poor, though I didn't know it at the time. My mother used to say, "God will provide," and He did.

Today the railroad is gone and my old hometown doesn't look the same. My son says, "Mom, that's progress." I don't think I like progress. At least not as well as I liked the old days.

Peggy Wolfe
Heber Springs, Ark.

Hobos

Old Smokey the Train

There is a big black engine and a little red caboose,
in the middle are a few boxcars that won't turn loose.
It goes huffing and puffing down the railroad track,
I don't know where it's going, but I know it will be back.
It leaves a long trail of smoke and lots of steam,
the men who run it make up a good team.
The engineer, fireman, conductor and a man to sweep the floor,
and don't forget the whistle blower.
It chugs along at a pretty good speed,
when you hear the whistle blowing, clear the crossing and
take heed.
It slows down going around the bend,
that is where the hobos jump on and get in.
They get off in some big town,
and spend a few days just bumming around.
To see Old Smokey going through the tunnels and
mountains out west,
is a beautiful picture at its best.
When it crosses the river on the trussel,
little boys grab their fishing poles and hustle.
Smoke blows and coal cinders fly,
they can really hurt when they get in your eye.
Old Smokey spent many years going from coast to coast,
carrying troops, passengers and freight to where it was
needed most.
The engineer keeps his hand on the throttle and his eye
on the track,
while the wheels go rumbling with a clicking and clack.
The fireman shovels on the coal –
that back-breaking job can get pretty old.
Old Smokey is now in its final resting place.
Now they use diesel trains to take its place.
Modern trains are probably the best,
but give me Old Smokey and you can have the rest.
Trains are like people, when they are old and outdated,
they are pushed aside and no longer related.
I'm glad that God has a place for everyone,
no matter how old or how young.

George Likley
Leesburg, Fla.

Chapter 8
Railroad Memories

Teresa remembers the Dinkey

The Dinkey was a small locomotive that ran between towns hauling freight during the week, in the 1920s. It hauled people on the weekends. That's when Teresa would go to the neighboring towns to shop for eggs, fresh milk and live poultry.

Her friends often made the trip with her because it was fun to "ride the rails." One of their trips got very exciting. They had finished their shopping and boarded the Dinkey for home. Teresa had a firm grip on the live chicken she carried under her arm, but the man who sold them the chicken had not tied its legs tightly enough, and the chicken got loose.

Teresa was in tears. The other girls tried to console her, but it did no good. She cried because she was afraid the chicken would fly through one of the open windows, and if they didn't have the chicken when they got home, they would have been punished.

The chicken flew all over the Dinkey. Everyone was hollering and trying to catch it. Finally, the conductor caught the scared bird. He tied its feet together securely and handed it back to Teresa, without smiling.

Everything worked out OK. Teresa never told her mother about the incident. Times have changed. No live chickens in shops and no Dinkey.

Catherine Berra Bleem
Sparta, Ill.

Takes me back

When I was a young girl, I lived in the small town of Powell, Texas. A passenger train came along the Cotton Belt Railway and stopped every evening at 11:45 p.m. That late night whistle meant a lot to me, not to mention my parents.

My parents were adamant that I had better be on the front porch by the time the train sounded its whistle, signaling the end of my date. At that time, I resented this rail monster dictating my curfew. But across the arc of time, what I would give to hear that train come rattling in just one more time.

The resounding rhythm of train wheels clicking in the darkness of the night always takes me back to my youth.

Faye Field
Longview, Texas

Special gift from the conductor

My family moved to a new farm in 1929, where I'm sure the nearby railroad was known as Fortsmith and Western. This was during the Depression and Dust Bowl days. Jobs were scarce and hobos were plentiful. I was almost 5 years old, and to watch that big noise maker roll by was really something for a little farm girl.

My big memory was five years later. Mother was our church delegate to a convention, which happened to be in the town my sister and her husband lived with their son. The baby was only about a month old. I was going to get to go along and ride the train.

When the time came for Mother and me to board, this man who worked for the railroad asked me how old I was. When I told him that I was 10, he reached into his pocket, pulled out a nickel, handed it to me and told me that if I always kept it, I would never be broke. He was the conductor and a very nice man.

When we got back home, Mother gave me the box my canary's feed came in and some cotton, and told me to put my nickel in there. Then we put it in her trunk where all important things were kept.

After I graduated from high school, I went to Cadet nurse's training for a year and a half, only to learn that I didn't want to be a nurse. So I joined the Navy Waves. With my nurse's training, I was sent to Corps school, then to the U.S. Naval Hospital.

I returned to Oklahoma in 1952, with my two sons, on the day Gen. Dwight D. Eisenhower became our president. My 6-year-old son was at his grandma and grandpa's house, and he ran inside screaming that the house was on fire. It burned completely. We lost a lot of valuable family treasures.

A few days later, I was standing in the room where Mother kept her trunk, and I happened to think about my nickel. I started digging in the ashes and realized the box was gone, along with the high school diplomas, etc. But lying there in its exact shape, with the date and printing still legible, was my train gift, my nickel, in perfect condition.

So in spite of the many years and the fire, it seems the conductor was right. I'm 76 years old now, and I'm still not broke! I still have the nickel that was given to me on my very first train ride, in 1934.

Mrs. Johnnie Douvillier
Jones, Okla.

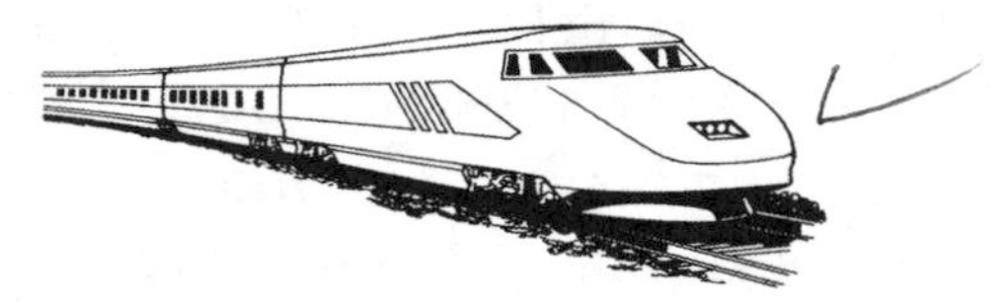

Shopping spree

Imagine our excitement – catching a train to go shopping on Saturday! Of course, this was about 1939, and our train, the Doodlebug, had only one car, as I remember.

We lived way out in the country and had no transportation. It was a real treat when the whole family got dressed in our Sunday best and waited for the train to take us to town. The conductor was a personal friend of my aunt's, so he always greeted us cheerfully.

The ride to town was thrilling for us children. We'd spend the morning looking at all of the fascinating displays in the shop windows. We'd have lunch at the dime store and then catch the latest cowboy movie, complete with popcorn and candy. Then it was time to catch the train home before it got dark.

I don't remember the names of any of the stores or the name of the movie theater. All I remember is that riding the Doodlebug was a highlight of my younger years.

Clydia DeFreese
Ruston, La.

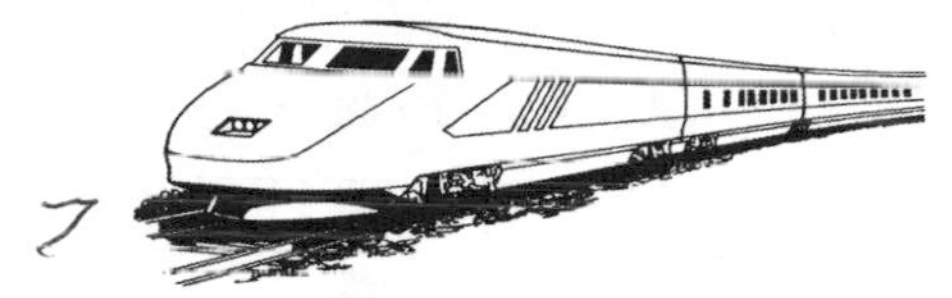

Me and the engineer

There have been many high points in my life that have left an unforgettable memory, and this one takes me back to early school years in the 1920s. I had not been in school long, when someone in my classroom became ill, and they sent our whole class home.

We lived on Lake Street, about a mile from town. To reach the main part of town from our house, you could either follow the road around the lake, or take a short cut by way of the railroad tracks. The tracks cut through the lake with a culvert to let the water flow freely between the small body of water and the large area of water, which was the lake proper. It was a lot shorter to walk the tracks instead of following the road, so most everyone on our street used this route to go to town, or for us to go to school.

Our town was a railroad center, so the one set of tracks entering town quickly spread out into six or eight sets going toward the round house and railroad station. We children always walked the back tracks when possible, as it was safer. They were less likely to be in use, and they came out where we could follow a path to the back of the school.

The day they sent our class home, I didn't know what I should do. I had never walked to or from school alone before. I thought I could go into my sister's room and wait for her, but they said I couldn't. So I bravely set out for home. About halfway there, I could hear the sound of an oncoming train. It was only an engine being used to make up a train in the yard.

Then I heard a man's voice.

"Little girl, what are you doing all alone?"

I told him what had happened, and he smiled.

"Who's your father?" he asked me, and I told him.

Then he surprised me by saying, "Come on, we're taking you home."

After helping me into the engine, they showed me around, explaining how they shoveled coal into the furnace to build up steam to run the engine. I stood beside him while we started up and drove down the tracks as far as the crossing.

"Do you know where you are now?" he asked, and I told him I did.

My father smiled when I told him about my adventure, for he knew the man who took me to the crossing.

But for a brief exciting time, there was only me, the engineer and that powerful engine.

Vera R. Houle
Troy, Mich.

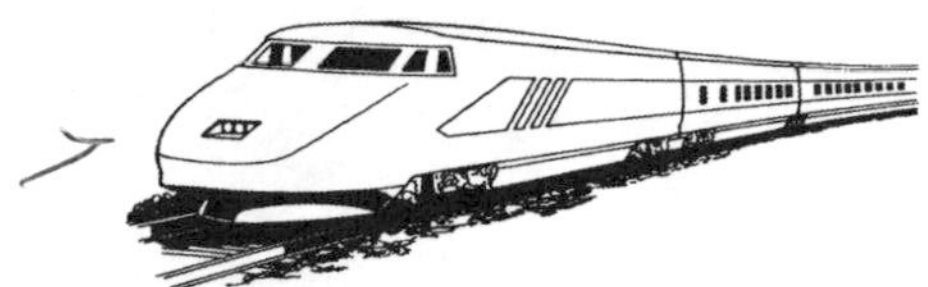

Price has increased

In the 1950s, a ticket to ride the Denver and Rio Grand from Canon City to Parkdale, Colo., through the Royal Gorge cost 35 cents per adult. We enjoyed taking relatives and out-of-town guests in the observation car with the glass dome, so they could see the Gorge.

The train stopped under the high suspension bridge and passengers were allowed to walk on the suspended foot bridge and view the big bridge overhead. When the train stopped at Parkdale for water, my husband would be waiting to take us home in the car.

We once took two exchange students from Colombia, South America, on this trip. Another time, we took two exchange students from Japan. They all enjoyed the thrill of that 11-mile train ride. We were sorry about passenger trains discontinuing that line altogether, in the mid-1960s, I believe.

Now a special train takes tourists on that same short trip, but you'd better believe the price is several times what we used to pay. But it was a wonderful experience.

Edythe Boston
Canon City, Colo.

INDEX

A

B

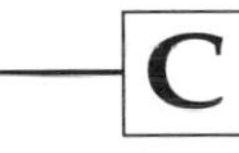

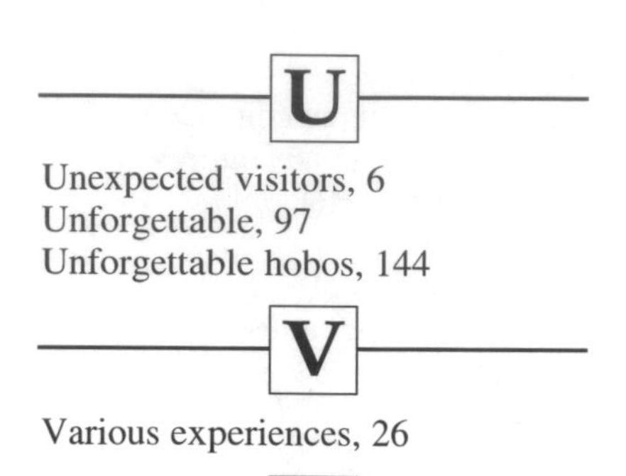

U

V

W

Y

Other titles in the My Folks series

My Folks Came In a Covered Wagon	1956
My Folks Claimed the Plains	1979
My Folks' Depression Days	1993
My Folks and the One-Room Schoolhouse	1993
My Folks and the Civil War	1994
My Folks and World War II	1994
My Folks Back to the Basics	1994
My Folks and the Land of Opportunity	1995

Ogden Publications wishes to acknowledge the following for their efforts in the editing and publication of this book: Ann Crahan, Diane Rader, Jean Teller and Cheryl Ptacek.